Can We Teach Ethics?

Can We Teach Ethics?

HOWARD B. RADEST

PRAEGER

New York
Westport, Connecticut
London

Library of Congress Cataloging-in-Publication Data

Radest, Howard B., 1928–
    Can we teach ethics? / Howard B. Radest.
        p.   cm.
    Bibliography: p.
    Includes index.
    ISBN 0-275-92857-8 (alk. paper)
    1. Ethics–Study and teaching (Secondary).   2. Ethics–Study and
teaching.   3. Ethical culture movement.   4. Moral education.
    5. Radest, Howard B., 1928–   .   I. Title.
    BJ66.R33 1989
    170'.7–dc 19   88–27512

Library of Congress Catalog Card Number: 88-27512
ISBN: 0-275-92857-8

First published in 1989

Praeger Publishers, One Madison Avenue, New York, NY 10010
A division of Greenwood Press, Inc.

Printed in the United States of America

The paper used in this book complies with the
Permanent Paper Standard issued by the National
Information Standards Organization (Z39.48–1984).

10 9 8 7 6 5 4 3 2 1

For

Rita,

Robert,

and

Michael

Contents

Introduction

About ten years ago, I was asked to consider a move from college teaching to school administration. One thing that interested me was the chance to do something about moral education. I'd thought of its problems, on and off, for some years as a teacher, as the leader of an Ethical Culture Society, and as a parent. I knew that the Ethical Culture/Fieldston Schools included an "ethics program" in its curriculum from 1st through 12th grades. I made the move.

I assumed, at first, that the answer to school problems was more effective curriculum. As a philosopher, the word and the idea were my realities, so solutions were to be found by using better words and getting clearer ideas. However, I soon found out that these would not do. There was another reality: the reality of students and teachers, and of institutional history and tradition. Somehow the philosopher's world and the school's world had to come together if moral education was to happen. That has been my project for the past decade. The outcome is reflected in this progress report, which is a sort of "pilgrim's progress."

Each chapter in this volume is a step along the way, although retrospect makes it all appear far more organized than it ever was in fact. I began as most of us do with some trust in moral common sense, but when a group of teachers asked me to talk about "moral education" and character, I was forced to reflect on their goal, the well-behaved student. As you will see, this turned out to be a problem and not a solution. I confess that this conclusion troubled me, but there it was.

Working in schools, you learn how little is under your control, particularly if you're supposed to be at the "top." Things happen that you don't expect; "little" decisions are made everywhere; students, parents, teachers, maintenance people, and secretaries bring their feelings and headaches into the place. Ways of doing things, scarcely acknowledged, impose limitations. In short, I discovered in experience what I had only known abstractly. Schools have their own culture, reflecting both their history and their environment. Obviously this is a commonplace, but now I felt it every day. Reflecting on the unintended led me to new concerns with the philosopher's question, "Can virtue be taught?" and with the answers we give. Hence, this resulted in the next steps along the way.

Most of all, I suppose, I learned a lesson that outsiders have trouble grasping. The truth about schools is found in the classroom. Now I should have learned this long ago, because my wife was a public school teacher for nearly 30 years, but I didn't. In fact, I had the typical intellectual bias that mistook erudition about subject matter for schooling. Teachers in two great elementary schools—the Midtown Ethical Culture School and the Fieldston Lower School—also taught me otherwise, and teachers at the Fieldston School showed me how the classroom and the "discipline" could be married effectively. I cannot help but add that my university colleagues have for the most part not yet learned the lesson.

I confess to frustration. Every time I started down the road to moral education, I had to go back to the classroom and found myself immersed in the fascinations of the unexpected. My goal kept getting farther and farther away, but perhaps that was the clue to finding answers to the question, "Can virtue be taught?" My colleagues in the Columbia University Seminar on Moral Education also pushed my thinking on that question. Other colleagues led me into the fascinations of Jean Piaget, Lawrence Kohlberg, and moral development. I found out that the curriculum wasn't as self-evident as I had thought. In fact, I found myself forced to parse it into at least five distinct curricula. Even more troubling, I also found that my rationalist bias didn't survive an analysis of what some have called the "implicit" curriculum. As it were, I was again diverted from the proper business of words and ideas.

Finally, I was led to the notion that the central fact of moral education was the act of teaching and not what was taught. Hence, a philosopher's intuitions about Socrates turned into rather more complicated notions of what it meant to be Socratic, and that, quite naturally, put me on to the relevance of theater to classroom. In the search for a suitable metaphor, I moved from dialogue as an austere and abstract dialectic—the philosopher's game—to dialogue as drama. The play and interplay of persons—that put moral education in the right place.

This unended odyssey taught me that no clear and distinct answer to a clear and distinct question exists. In fact, if I am correct, there can be no final wisdom on the subject, only an invitation to go on with the adventure. Two philosophic strands thus corrected my pedagogical naivete. Moral education is in the doing, and in the doing we stumble upon intrusions that have to be lived through and that cannot be predicted or disciplined. A certain existential pragmatism sets the climate for the more limited utility of reason.

II

In writing this book, I have tried to keep the readers in mind. Reading is a transaction between the author and the reader or, as Emerson remarked in *The American Scholar*, reading is a creative activity. Once the words are put out there, they take on a life of their own. Every reader is an author and recreates the text. I think that this exposes our natural affinity for dialogue and that any text is an invitation to speech.

Our subject, ethics, is about human relationships and their moral qualities. Since we continue to surprise each other—both pleasantly and otherwise—the process for keeping up with experience is as germane as the product. Talking seriously about moral education, then, expects the talk to go on. I suppose that is what bothers me about most ethics texts; they make going on difficult because they seem to say by what is written down that ethics has a beginning, middle, and end. Instead, this essay is an invitation to renew the discussion that is at the heart of moral education and to go on doing so.

Obviously, I've had lots of help, but, just as obviously, the use of it is my own. Early on, I benefitted from great teaching. The late Joseph Blau of Columbia was a lifelong mentor and friend. The late Lawrence Kohlberg in the all-too-brief years of our friendship never disappointed my need for both criticism and support. My colleagues in the Ethics Department of the Ethical Culture/Fieldston Schools were a constant source of information and insight. Other colleagues in the Association for Moral Education never let a philosopher forget the realities of the human psyche. Above all, the students I got to know taught me much more than I could ever teach them. I had constant evidence of what truly great teaching was all about when my wife would come home with stories of the classroom and during the ever-present nightly hours of thought and preparation for the next day. My sons, moving into their business careers, never let me forget the moral dilemmas of the world in which they were living. Consequently, I had lots of help.

I hold no brief for the wisdom of this progress report. It is, for now, the best I can say about what I've seen, heard, and done. If sharing this moves you to your own learning in your own way, then the effort is its reward. I learned from my teachers that they did not seek imitation but rather creation and recreation. If I learned my lesson well, then this essay should be a stimulus to reflection and not repetition. That, at least, is my hope, and I suspect that the process widely and generously shared is finally the way for moral education to happen.

Can We Teach Ethics?

1

The Well-Behaved Student:
Teaching Ethics

I

I've never really met a "well-behaved" student—I suppose none of us really has. However, I do want to think about our moral expectations, and the idea of a "well-behaved" student exposes those expectations. Of course, I've met the student who seems "well-behaved"—a "teacher's pet" or a "grind" or, more charitably, "a kid who doesn't make trouble," or "a good" boy or girl—and I've surely met their opposites. As a parent and teacher I very much want a "well-behaved" student to exist, and I do not think I am alone. This desire sometimes fools me into thinking he or she does in fact exist, and again I do not think I am alone. Expectations and appearances, hopes and doubts—teaching ethics is caught in illusions. Consequently, when I prepare an end-of-year "report card," I reveal myself as much as my student. Obedient, cooperative, cheerful; he or she "works and plays well with others," hands in homework assignments on time, always raises a hand and speaks up in class, is polite and lives by the rules, and gets good grades. In short, a joy to parents, a comfort to teachers, and a boon to administrators.

However, when I think about it, I grow a bit uneasy. I know what I want and I know when I don't get it. In fact, it's easy enough to find the failures. I suspect myself and my judgements, however, when I finally put these ideal characteristics together in a "profile" and then "grade" a student on them as "excellent" or "satisfactory." Are the successes and failures really that different? Surely this paragon, like his or her opposite, must have his or her angers, moments of deceit, uncharitable thoughts, but these do not show up or, when they do, they surprise me, which suggests that something is hidden or is hiding. When I can figure out why this complicated interplay exists, I will also find out something of what moral education is all about.

I begin with the trust and love on which relationships between parent and child, teacher and student are built. When I think of the "well-behaved" student, however, I suspect that these are replaced by relationships of authority and power. At the same time, I cannot admit it, because I want to believe that good behavior flows from trust and love. When it does not, the anxiety I already feel in facing children increases. They seem so quickly to grow up, to learn to mask themselves, and to become a mystery to me, so, as with other anxieties, I suppress my doubts and fears. Beneath a surface approval, the idea of a "well-behaved" student thus becomes a focus of tensions.

The "well-behaved" student exhibits the commonsense virtues, but in experience, events force moral conflicts on us. Moral realities come at us with alarming rapidity and troubling novelty. Still, I am comforted by the familiar values I meet in the "well-behaved" student, and thus am tempted to confuse moral continuity with changelessness. The "well-behaved" student becomes an ambiguous figure, but I go on trying to describe him or her in unambiguous language. Intention, image, and experience separate. Since this is an open secret, trust in myself, and between myself and my students is eroded.

To preserve the fictions of this familiar morality, I try to keep the world away from my children, but my motives are mixed. Of course, I love my child, my student, but I am also protecting myself. I succeed in this strategy because I am an adult. I enjoy the natural confidence of the young, and, since a child's readiness to take in the world needs time to develop, I can also justify this use of my powers. However, like all adults, I extend these powers well beyond infancy, and this is not merely a personal preference but a social and cultural strategy as well. We reveal ourselves collectively by what we say about our families and schools, and by what we count as their successes and failures. In short, I think we all want to find or to create the "well-behaved" student, but preliminary reflection already opens us and it to question.

II

Schooling tempts us to protect by isolation, but isolation fails. A teacher brings the world into the classroom; a student will be heard. Still we persist in trying to keep the world away. Symptomatically, we treat books as agents of corruption, and typically we suspect teachers of a conspiracy against innocence.[1]

Isolation can even seem effective. We set up the school—for good reasons it seems to us—to be distant from and unlike learning and practice everywhere else, and then it boomerangs. Students learn that school lacks connections to their experience. Many—as in urban high schools—drop out or play truant. Others develop a "nonaggression" pact with us, so to speak, a treaty between "well-behaved" teenagers and disappointed teachers.[2] Successful performance on tests and the like allows these students to survive by meeting our expectations. We, in turn, survive by indulging the illusion that schooling can be reduced to standard performances, but these expectations confuse appearance with reality. For example, criticism of standard tests like "SATs" is commonplace. We know how little they have to do with what counts as schooling, as education. Complaint about their superficiality and about the dangers of competition for admission to the "right" colleges among our better students is routine, but we do not change.

Within the school, we try to sterilize experience. Sex, death, and violence are inescapably present in history, literature, and biology, yet we put these out of the classroom and then wonder why our students "tune out." By way of illustration, compare our textbooks with our streets. Daily our children pass scenes of variety, energy, beauty, ugliness, and violence on the way to or from the school, but in the classroom, most of the time, it is as if none of what was seen, heard, or felt had happened. Of course, there are reasonable distinctions between sensationalism and description, between titillation and characterization. Unfortunately, we neglect the latter two in order to avoid the former. What we miss, ironically, is the chance to develop moral and aesthetic standards that would help us to make the distinctions.

Teachers, of course, know the link between biography and classroom, but their efforts to build on the relationships of personality and curriculum are seldom encouraged. Instead, we look for "teacherproof" curricula. Those teachers who persist in their individuality become objects of aggression and criticism by politicians, administrators, PTAs, and even colleagues. The pressure for rigidity increases, the more anxious we become. Thus, the epidemic of reports on schools in the 1980s—beginning with the National Committee on Excellence in Education's *A Nation at Risk* in 1983—has elevated our love affair with quantification and accountability to idolatry. The resulting dissatisfaction of teachers so widely reported these days is not simply a matter of money or status. It is connected very deeply with our demand that they conform to irrelevance. For example, the move toward "basic" skills, that is, skills without context, is a move toward morally "safe" subject matters.[3] It is not accidental that this move recurs as a fundamentalist climate increases in intensity. The ongoing quarrel about "sex education" is a paradigm of protectiveness. Of course, we both know and deny that sexual experience, pregnancy, and abortion are no stranger to the child, and the examples multiply as we call for a "return to God in the schools" in a poorly disguised effort to make teachers and students toe the mark, or as we focus on "discipline" or drug addiction as the sole problem for national educational policy.[4] Since we cannot really keep the school hidden from the world, our anxiety in the presence of the young only increases. Consequently, as with other anxieties, we redouble our protective efforts even as they fail, and we grow even more uneasy.

Our uneasiness has other sources, too. Many of us really want our students to acquire a permanent store of moral habits, to be "well-behaved." Paradoxically, we then isolate schooling from the realities of marriage, politics, business, and work-life. We also assume that punctuality, cooperativeness, loyalty, obedience, and truth telling are sufficient for a moral life in the world, yet we cannot close the book on virtue simply by training for "good" habits. For example, the moral structure of compromise, without which a democratic politics becomes impossible, is missing. The businessman trying to judge whether an act is bribery or not and what to do about it cannot rely on the lessons of childhood. The move from romance to marriage calls for a nicety of judgement for which moral habits are simply inadequate.

In fact, what we set out to do in order to get a "well-behaved" student reminds us of infant rearing. We train babies to do many useful things like sleeping through the night, eating solid foods, and using the toilet, but we also want to help the child leave infancy. Intelligence, freedom, and even a praiseworthy stubbornness appear as we grow up. Relationships become more complicated, yet when we condemn our schools to moral behaviorism, we suppress the thought that the child is leaving infancy behind. In other words, we try to achieve moral success, the "well-behaved" student, in an unambiguous way despite the ambiguities of growing up.

In seeking the "well-behaved" student, we presume that we know what the moral life is all about. For this to be so, someone must decide what counts as virtue, what goes into this "bag of virtues", and in what order.[5] Moral conflicts arise, moral decisions are needed, and moral authority is exercised. Another source of uneasiness appears because we do not help our "well-behaved" student to judge between moral and immoral authority. In fact, he or she is to be trained to grant moral authority or status as such, that is, to teachers as teachers, parents as parents.[6] This makes the "habit of obedience" the first virtue. We hear it in the nostalgia of parents or teachers who long for the "good old days" when "kids knew their place." At the same time, we surely know the moral outrage that follows the statement: "I was only obeying orders."

Our "well-behaved" student is to be taught that moral issues are taken care of by good habits, yet it is no mystery to anyone that virtues collide. Few students are ignorant of the conflict between loyalty to a friend and "telling tales," nor can any of us know in advance where and how moral conflict will appear. To be sure, we are helped by a reservoir of history. Everything cannot change all the time without threatening our moral sanity. However, things do change, and so we cannot avoid moral inquiry, but the "well-behaved" student is not to inquire.

Hiding behind our "well-behaved" student is a view of the proper place of children and other "lesser beings." The stuff of morality is really an adult responsibility. Schooling is a form of transmission from adult to child. Childhood is in a strange way amoral, consisting of an obedience to other people's rules. Moral education, like all education, is finally preparatory.

This radical separation between adults and children seems reasonable until we realize that it violates our sense of what counts as moral and our beliefs about who can be moral. After all, we expect children not only to tell the truth or help a friend but to choose to do so. Moral responsibility presumes this ability to choose, the ability to evaluate alternatives and set priorities. By contrast, when we reserve to adults the power to set the rules—which is what makes for a "well-behaved" student—moral experience takes on an arbitrary character. The student is thus a product of trying to do moral education in a nonmoral way. As a result, we only increase moral confusion.

Symptomatically, a separation between practice and ethics emerges as the sign of growing up. Adults say and believe that morality has "nothing to do with" business, law, or politics. A deadly dualism evolves. In public life, "results" count. Love and goodness abide, if at all, in the special relations of family and tribe. Moral choices as live options vanish from the public and social life. Our rhetoric becomes only moralistic, and ethics finally has little place in our experience. The student reads this as the hypocrisy of adults, as anyone who has worked with teenagers can testify. Sadly, this dualism is not so much hypocrisy as the surrender of morality itself. Psychologically, intimacy cannot be sustained in isolation, so even intimacy succumbs to opportunism.

As I reflect on these preliminary notes about what we try to do in the name of schooling, I am not surprised that the idea of the "well-behaved" student makes me uncomfortable. I express this discomfort by making the idea an object of "hidden" derision. It is a commonplace of the faculty room to indulge in no little scepticism about those who appear to be "well-behaved" students, nor is it envy alone that leads other students to sneer at them. Their parents at an "open school evening" enjoy the glow of praise and yet, knowing the reality about their children, also feel the worry of unsureness. Typically, it is these parents who show up over and over again at such events almost ritualistically asking for assurance. Finally, students, knowing the moral emptiness of the lessons learned in the cause of becoming "well-behaved," turn to a destructive cynicism.

III

Of course, a "well-behaved" student will also be a complicated and growing human being. Proposed as an object in two dimensions and met with praise and suspicion, the idea and its approximations in experience cannot help but increase mistrust of adults as students grasp the gulf that exists between our rhetoric and their moral experience. At the same time we create this model of adult approval, we isolate it from actual student life. Our "well-behaved" student would thus be trebly alienated: from adults who take the pose for the reality; from peers who resent adult manipulation; and from a self that exhibits the shallowness of doing without knowing or understanding what is going on, yet none of this can be admitted.

It's very strange. The "well-behaved" student is not to know what good behavior is all about. To know is to hesitate, to interrupt, to question, to judge, and above all to risk mistakes. On the other hand, our student will succeed by becoming morally passive, by making our moral ends into his or her "good" habits. We thus deny to him or her the space for moral reflection, criticism, and intelligence, since this would interfere with the effectiveness of those habits. Once we called this "molding [*sic*] character"; today we talk about "socialization." Both views assume that virtues are transmitted by morally privileged authorities to uninitiated others. Both assume that morality is for most people finally summed up in arbitrary rules. Although the old and the new views may seem to be antagonists, they are one in adopting a reductive view of moral education. While the former looks to the commandments of tradition and the latter to the directives of social science, both conceive of schooling as training.

Both old and new views take a nonmoral view of virtue itself. For the older way, moral rules are given by nature or by God, and speak of "revelation." For the newer way, moral rules are social conventions like "rules of the road." It is typical to speak of conditioning. In both cases, moral conduct is produced by a suitable balance of praise and punishment. Moral questions are simply questions of fact—theological, metaphysical, sociological, or psychological. Our "well-behaved" student may even be expected to learn a bit of moral history or how to use standard justifications like "It is God's will," or "It avoids car crashes." He or she is to learn moral rules in the same way as he or she learns the location of the continents or the name of the first president of the United States—and often with the same lack of depth.[7] The painful subjectivity of judgement, the joys and struggles of reflection presented to us in moral situations are absent.

In its newer costume, socialization enjoys an added advantage: it is "scientific." We use the language of the culture, even moral language itself, as part of conditioning, but this is merely a technical device. In another time and in another place we might have used some other language to achieve the same ends, for example, the language of piety or of national loyalty. However, at bottom, this conditioning can leave no room for understanding what is moral about approved conduct other than the fact that it is approved. To the young it appears as an exercise of power; for the adult, it simply eliminates morality as a relevant category of experience.

For example, "student government" in most schools is a telltale of adult control and student passivity. Little that is important is at stake. It is simply another way to go through the motions and be rewarded by adults. Students humor us when they join in, but they are not really fooled. Instead, they build a second world with its special language, costume, and symbol. Adults are excluded. In that world, students experience realities of sexuality and friendship, and maneuver for economic goods and political control. Not surprisingly, this second world looks very much like the first world on which it is modeled, that is, imitation unexamined makes this second world also amoral. True, moments of idealism may appear, but a reversion to cliquishness and manipulation is never far away. Ultimately, power remains with the adult world. At extreme moments—for example, youth gangs, a "drug culture"—the two worlds engage in debilitating warfare. Of course, the adult world wins, although at great cost. It is this pattern of imitation and not the so-called permissiveness of the progressives that really produces the demoralization and anomie we complain of in our children.

Adulthood comes to be defined by the fact that it can impose its will, make its judgements stick. To be grown-up is not a matter of wisdom or sensitivity but of the effective exercise of power. We may argue an issue with our children, but we will win because we are adults. Resentment in the relationships between young and old is therefore not surprising. Even more troubling, resentment comes to be associated with morality itself. When we were young, we had to learn our morals as adult-enforced prohibitions. The "well-behaved" student reminds us that the pattern continues.

There is something peculiarly modern about our image of the aims for which a "well-behaved" student is the means. Despite the violence in many of our schools, a cool, noncontroversial, success-oriented adult is the typical achievement of modern culture. The so-called "yuppie" is a moral paradigm. Criticism and challenge to authority are muted. Only the "outsiders" act up, and then really do so in order to be invited inside, so the "successful" urban high school finds ways of promising worldly reward. Since, in our culture, this is typically monetary, we find some schools paying "poor" students for attendance, for taking tests, for getting passing grades. It is not surprising that "scholarships" are used as surrogates for "pay-offs," most notably, but not only, in sports. The success of minority-group athletes is thus morally ambivalent, praiseworthy as opportunity and troubling as betrayal. The "civil rights" movement, the "women's movement" measure their success by achieving what the "other" culture has achieved. The few voices that deny the self-evident value of admission to that "other" culture are heard as alien and unintelligible. The "radicals" of the 1960s become bankers and stockbrokers. The underclasses act out of resentment; they have not been given the rewards of good habits. The children of the liberal community live in this world and, at the same time, reject it by moving toward orthodoxy, esoteric sects, or indifference.

IV

Nonetheless, I can understand why parents, teachers, and politicians are tempted by moral conditioning. Behavior can be described and measured, and this meets today's prejudice. We are, however, reflective animals. We have feelings; we reason about goals, purposes, ideals. To find out about these, we have to infer, guess, interpret. We cannot be sure that the answers we get are accurate. These answers may also be outcomes of manipulation, ways of getting "good behavior" as many a classroom inhabited by popular teachers reveals. Certainly reflection implicates our own feelings, reasons, and purposes, our own ability to be truthful and to know what the truth is. However, these are always problematic; we can never be sure that they are our own. The difficulties within difficulties of moral education can become oppressive in their uncertainty. The "well-behaved" student seems to avoid these uncertainties but at the cost of acquiring an unintelligible morality.

There are many possible reasons that can be given for the same behavior. Only some of them, however, are moral reasons. For example, our "well-behaved" student is helpful to others. When asked, he or she is to recite a moral rule: to be helpful is to be good. We discover—perhaps by listening to students who appear to come close to our idea—that this means that to be good is to do what is pleasing to teachers. We listen further and find out that what is pleasing to teachers shows up in good grades, nice words to parents, recommendations for honors. Withhold the good grade, forget the nice words, or shift the locus of authority, and our students show another face. They come to the teacher to bargain for the withheld "good." Failing that, they grow angry and retreat mumbling about the unfairness of it all. An uncharacteristic silence in the classroom is heard from places where once hands waved vigorously and frequently. In short, we encourage opportunism in the guise of moral education.

Even our observations of behavior entail their own paradox and are unreliable. Our students may be using "good" behavior as a way of dealing with adults, but we do not know. Out of sight, they behave one way in school, another way at home, still another way on the street, yet we cannot observe these other spaces, and so cannot know what is going on. Our presence as parents or as teachers changes things. It comes as a shock, for example, when a student we thought was "well-behaved" cheats or steals. Newspaper accounts of a crime typically report the "surprise" of the criminal's neighbors.

Teachers know that students will use "good conduct" to get non-moral rewards—not always, but often enough to suggest the moral unreliability of "good conduct." Good grades are all too often tokens of successful negotiation, at least as often as of effective study. We admit this, for example, when we organize courses in "test taking" and call the outcomes, with unintended irony, "survival techniques," and we teachers are praised for the achievements of our "good" students. Since we too are prudential animals, we keep our silences. At the same time, we are uneasy because we know that despite the appearance of virtue, our students can as readily be manipulators as moralists. Our praise of a "well-behaved" student is an invitation to opportunism; our praise of a teacher for his or her "well-behaved" students is an invitation to cynicism—and all in the name of character.

We notice a move toward "realism" as students move from kindergarten to graduate school, that is, toward an environment closer to the world outside. Not surprising is the fact that we call graduate study "trade school" and the doctorate a "union card." Not surprising either is the anger of teachers at a society that betrays us. We did not enter the classroom to become cynics or to shape opportunists, yet we too must blind ourselves to our own acquiescence, even our complicity, in order to survive. Our anger is suppressed and teaching comes to be accompanied by resentment. Because suppressed, its causes are lost and we find other objects for our angers. Faculties are thus filled with tension, and are often bitter and sad. Again, the lack of financial reward and social status is not a sufficient explanation for the dismay that attends life in schools. After all, these were well known before we chose to be teachers. However, the secret of our silences only comes to us later, if at all, and, some would say "too late."

As we grow older, we are encouraged to surrender moral values to more pressing demands. We and our schools conspire to say that morality is for the innocent only. Career and success come to count above all else. At the same time, we are helpless to do anything but reward "good" conduct as long as we accept the premises that create the "well-behaved" student. The idea reminds us that protectiveness is an illusion, but we must deny that it is illusory. We realize that our "well-behaved" student is simultaneously a product of infantilist training and adult surrender.

The difference between claim and conduct haunts us. We know that helpfulness out of concern for another is not morally the same as helpfulness for payment. We know that truth telling out of respect for accuracy is not morally the same as truth telling for fear of being caught in a lie. In short, simply to equate "good" behavior with morality doesn't make sense. To approach moral education through behavior raises questions that are unanswerable except by leaving behavior behind just because it rules out feelings, reasons, and ends except as patterned items of conduct.

V

Given suitable strategies of reward and punishment, "well-behaved" students are almost an achievable goal—I say, "almost" because thankfully human beings are stubborn enough and contrary enough to subvert even the best of schemes. Thus we have the self-congratulatory stories of reformed urban schools when a "tough" principal takes over. By selecting appropriate content for behavior like classroom decorum and economic success, we can even achieve social utility. Moral reflection, on the other hand, is hesitant. Above all, moral knowledge is only loosely coupled to moral behavior, and yet one without the other turns morality into a charade. We've all "known" the right thing to do but have not done it. We've known what to do and done its opposite. Moral intelligence even at its best works imperfectly. The connections between intent, motive, and action remain elusive. By contrast, even if behavior does not carry its own moral credentials, at least it is clear and useful. In very difficult environments, its achievement is not lightly dismissed.

However, knowing, feeling, and reasoning do make a moral difference, and it is not very sensible to reduce moral education to successful conditioning or social control. We do distinguish between inadvertent and intentional wrongdoing; informed and uninformed judgement. Sometimes we tell the truth because it's the "right thing" to do; sometimes because it gets us what we want; sometimes because it helps or hurts someone we like or dislike. These are three distinct acts of truth telling, although the "behavior" that we observe is the same.

Even when our students can give moral reasons for moral acts, the moral situation poses further difficulty. Perhaps our students are conforming to social expectations in an environment where "giving reasons" is expected, for example, in the intellectualistic climate of a college preparatory high school. The question, "Why did you do that?" calls forth skills of reasonable argument, and we can teach those skills. We can even test for student competence in their use with suitable questionnaires, instruments that measure "attitudes," tests of mathematical reasoning, and so forth. Once again, however, reward and punishment are at work. Our students may well be moved by the pleasure of being praised for intellectual conformity or the fear of being punished for nonconformity. Ironically, the brighter our students are, the more effectively moral indifference can be masked by the ability to generate "reasons." We recognize failures of moral education even where moral reasons are given by calling it sophistry in advance of the event or rationalization after the event. In other words, reason needs a moral commitment to reasoning and is never simply an abstract skill.

Our students, then, may be said to be well-behaved and even morally skilled and yet lack passion and empathy, which are states of being and not actions. They may not "care" or, more accurately, on behavioral grounds we cannot know that they care; we can only observe conduct that may—or may not—flow from caring. Since moral cognitions are not simply rational exercises, they remain a puzzle for moral psychology. "Good" conduct and "good" reasons may simply be motivated by a desire for the comfort of avoiding moral conflict. Alas, when truly skilled, our students may even perform the drama of moral passion quite effectively too; again this presents the problem of appearance and reality.

The idea of the "well-behaved" student hides another problem. He or she may, under certain conditions, be indistinguishable from a "badly behaved" student. A moral act is important not only for its own sake but because it verifies what is otherwise the report of an interested party; in other words, my report of my intentions and feelings is always biased. However, if we look only to conduct, we are left morally dumb when action is impossible. For example, I want to save a drowning man but cannot swim and so I do not jump into the water. I thus appear to be passive, but a moral choice may have been made. A student may thus be either morally praiseworthy or blameworthy, and we have no way of deciding which it is. Indifference is not morally the same as helplessness.

The more we probe the characteristics of the "well-behaved" student, the more problematic the idea becomes. We couple responsibility with autonomy. Where choice is impossible, culpability ends. Consequently, we must know to what extent a student is acting on incomplete or misleading information and to what extent that information was intentionally shaped by others. Autonomy is particularly problematic for the young. We impose adult expectations often without realizing what we're doing. Educational and vocational goals are inculcated in the young by parent and culture at an early age. A student may be cooperative, literate, rational, and so forth—but even reason giving and feelings are often coerced, and often unintentionally so. We come upon a most troubling and puzzling feature of moral education. We cannot open up all choices to the young and deny all authority to the adult as in some parodies of progressivism. How then ought adults to exercise their evident powers in a morally legitimate way and how are the young to be equipped to distinguish between legitimate and illegitimate limitations and impositions? In schools, this question is posed by the distinction between education and indoctrination, and raises the issue of developmental readiness. On the other hand, when we settle for "good" habits out of despair at resolving issues of moral authority, we fail to acknowledge the freedom that a moral life requires.

VI

We have been looking at moral education using an individualistic image: the "well-behaved" student, but that is finally inadequate on yet other grounds. Students exist in environments and environments affect students. An adequate account needs to look at class and status, ethnic history, sexuality, religious commitment, and family structure. Even without these further complications, we can already see that "good" behavior cannot by itself be a pedagogical ideal. Once we admit that even "reason giving" and "feelings" may be outcomes of conditioning or of training, we are driven to issues of reflection. When we also admit that moral competence is in part a derivation of locations in time, space, and history, we cannot settle for a single set of fixed moral laws applicable now and forever, to young and to old, here and everywhere. Our idea had better be pluralized; there needs to be more than one kind of "well-behaved" student. Soon, however, the kinds become numerous enough to challenge the usefulness of the idea itself.

The complexity and richness of the moral situation is unsuccessfully suppressed in the idea of the "well-behaved" student. The questions, concerns, and puzzles stirred up by the "well-behaved" student are in fact the subject of often uncritical but continuing discussion among those of us who work with the young. Unable to calm our uneasiness, we welcome almost any offering of solution. That, in large measure, accounts for the fashions that infect moral education. Fads appear and disappear with alarming rapidity, and the field itself often takes on the appearance of party politics.

Complicating the effort to find sensible pedagogies are the political climate, the pressures of sectarianism, the demands of parents, and our penchant for a "quick fix." Complicating it even further is the illusion that anyone can be a moral expert. In an environment so charged with partisan interests and anxious responses, it is no wonder that defensive postures are the norm. Teachers are thus given to an excessive classroom pragmatism, while scholars do their research in almost deliberate ignorance of the classroom. What we learn from pilot studies and "model" schools is seldom translated into an available practice. When it is, as with "values clarification"[8] and "philosophy for children,"[9] it is embraced with passionate relief but then rejected since it offers no final answers. Finally, a current of anti-intellectualism infects much of the life of schooling. Resistance from many quarters and not least of all from within the school itself then is a condition to be overcome in any effort to achieve good sense about moral education.

At the same time, nostalgia for "getting back" to moral values in schooling and for exhibiting these in "well-behaved" students are fueled by a genuine concern. The modernist push toward "science" in all things has nurtured the illusion of value-free knowledge and moral behaviorism. The need for a common schooling in a pluralistic society has too often turned toleration into indifference and indifference into ignorance. By reflecting on a familiar phenomenon of desire, the "well-behaved" student, an agenda emerges. We expose the structures of our uneasiness about moral education, revealing a ground toward which teacher, researcher, parent, and citizen can move, that is, the reestablishment of trust and love, the uses of reason, the curb of power, and the confession of moral riskiness. The first step is taken when we grasp the fact that the "well-behaved" student is a problem and not a solution.

Notes

1. A typical example:

A popular author of books for young people charged last week that the problem of censorship in American society is growing more serious. It makes authors fearful of writing "realistic" books for the young said Norma Klein, who noted she had experienced attempts to suppress a number of her 40 novels for young adults.

In Anne Bridgman, "Censors Increasingly Attacking 'Realistic' Books, Author Says," *Education Week*, Washington, D.C. (September 19, 1984): 10.

2. I am indebted to Theodore Sizer, Dean, School of Education, Brown University, who in his recent book, *Horace's Compromise* (Boston: Houghton Mifflin, 1984) describes that "nonaggression" relationship in a number of the high schools he visited for his study.

3. The back to basics movement in education that began in the 1970's has succeeded in assuring that almost every American high school graduate can handle simple mathematics, new testing data released yesterday suggested. But the data show that virtually no progress has been made in developing more complicated mathematical skills. . . . The results confirmed trends apparent in a study of students' reading capabilities released earlier this year.

In Edward B. Fiske, "Schools' Back to Basics Drive Found To Be Working In Math," *The New York Times*, June 8, 1988.

4. For example, the 1984 Republican Party Platform on education called for a return to "basics," the right to "voluntary prayer," increased competition to be encouraged by items such as tuition tax credits, and, using the language of

local control and parental responsibility, it clearly intends a return to a traditional, authority-based, academically narrow schooling. We do not expect this attitude to change since it is indeed representative of the public mood.

5. The late Lawrence Kohlberg, director of the Center for Moral Education at Harvard University, used the phrase, "a bag of virtues" to describe traditional collections of moral "goods" that have simply accrued without an organizing principle or attention to moral and cognitive development. A familiar example—and one to which Kohlberg often referred—is the Boy Scout "law," that is, "A Scout is trustworthy, loyal, . . ."

6. In the course of the "Iran-Contra" Hearings (Congress of the United States, Washington D.C., July 4–10, 1987), the paradigm description of the vices of virtue was exhibited by Lieutenant-Colonel Oliver North. Deception, lying, misappropriation of funds—all of these vanished as relevant moral categories. The issue for Colonel North was reduced to authority and obedience. Public nostalgia for such moral simplemindedness was illustrated by the immediate support from the public reported in a number of opinion polls. Fortunately, as time passed, reflection apparently eroded that support.

7. Consider the revealing and direct statement put by B. F. Skinner in his book, *Beyond Freedom and Dignity* (New York: Knopf, 1971), which maintains that virtue is to be replaced by scientifically validated behavioral goals achieved by experimentally developed conditioning techniques.

8. "Values clarification" is a methodology and pedagogy developed by Louis Raths, Merrill Harmin, and Sidney Simon, which is widely used in public schools both because it is readily available to the classroom and because it appears to meet the needs of moral education and pluralistic tolerance. (See chapter 4.)

9. Another widely used program is that of Matthew Lippman's "philosophy for children" developed at his center in Montclair, New Jersey. (See chapter 4.)

2

Can Virtue Be Taught?
The Problem of Moral Education

I

The "well-behaved" student would be unable to make the Socratic confession, "I know that I know nothing," and like him or her, we too have trouble in confessing the moral ambiguity in our experience. Our hunger for moral safety is overwhelming, yet to make moral sense, we need to admit our ignorance. As old as Athens, the confession is as new as the moment around the dinner table or in the classroom when our children—as children will—confront us with contraditions between our talk and our practice. They remind us of what we know and do not know.

However, not all ignorance is Socratic. Ignorance can be an escape or an alibi. We easily confuse it with innocence, and confuse innocence with moral wisdom. To be sure, the Christmas story or *Alice in Wonderland* have their charms, but we will not find our way by becoming children again. Sometimes, too, ignorance is only a pose. We adopt it in order to invite others to praise our moral modesty or use it to surrender to authority. Thus we want to believe the despot who claims he is a "servant" of the people. We "escape from freedom."[1] By contrast, moral ignorance leads to interesting questions and to the exercise of moral curiosity, but this curiosity only seems childlike.

At the same time, moral ignorance is only part of the story. If we knew nothing at all, we could not even ask questions. For example, someone lies to us. We feel disturbed. Something is wrong and someone is wronged. We find that we already have a moral vocabulary to

17

voice that disturbance. Somehow we already knew that "telling the
truth" was right; "hurting people" was wrong; "being friendly" was
right; "cheating" was wrong—and lots of other things too. Thus, we
know that we know nothing and we also know what's right and
wrong.

Our moral knowledge is established in us very early in life, and is
made up of habits learned before they are named and described. However, habits only work in familiar environments. They are stretched
and broken when moral rules come into conflict with each other or
when environments grow alien. Things happen of which the rules do
not speak. What was dependable grows shaky. The world, finally, has
a way of forcing us to take account of it in unexpected ways.

Still, we try very hard to hold on to our habits even if their guid-
ance is contradictory and confusing. We pull back from moral ignorance, but the moral neighborhood is in motion and so we get trapped
into irrelevant debates and talk past each other. This is all the more
annoying and frustrating, so we raise our voices, repeat our catalogue
of virtues and vices, and call even more loudly for a "return" to
moral values. Of course, the interesting questions don't go away.
They continue to pique our curiosity even when we don't want to
admit it.

Sometimes we try to shift to the political arena, thinking to resolve
ambiguity by overpowering the enemy. We mount campaigns against
"relativism" or "dogmatism," but that doesn't work either. In fact,
the liberal, more often than not, agrees with the traditionalist about
day-to-day moral rules. Both are concerned with conscience and conscientiousness, with integrity and honesty. Issues arise between
them—and similarly between secularists and religionists—when the
"how" and "where" of judgment become problematic. Who shall
decide and on what grounds when values conflict, when events do not
fit inherited wisdoms, or when the meanings of integrity, honesty, or
what have you are blurred?

Frequently the moral rules need only to be amended, and more
rarely to be invented. Our cognitive armory—analogy, comparison, or
generalization—comes into play. We try to find out whether the past
is usable, and it often is, but sometimes analogies are false, comparisons weak, or generalizations inadequate. Then we are forced to the
moral imagination against our will.

The politics and the psychology of virtue work against using our
imaginations. We prefer the claims of authority against the uncer-

tainties of creation. At least someone "knows" the good and, what is even more comforting, someone accepts responsibility. The burden of choice is lifted from us. Understandably too, we feel the need of moral security just because the consequences of moral failure are seldom trivial, so we suspect the moral imagination and try to deny that we really encounter moral novelty. We try to restrict conscience to the application of moral rules. Of course that doesn't work. We are returned to moral ignorance.

At least these quarrels between liberal and conservative are carried on in good faith. On the other hand, some people are really after control over others, and morality is a superb tool of control. Others may not even realize the move from virtue to power, since nothing comes more easily to us than the thought, "I know what's best for you." We heard the claim over and over again when we were children. We had to obey and we resented it, yet we could hardly admit this resentment openly, for to do so would give love the lie. Consequently, morality acquired a hostile tone very early in our lives, and this still underlies the angers of the moral life. Hence, the question itself, "Can virtue be taught?" comes to be felt as a threat and an invasion, and a reminder of our helplessness.

Our values reflect and are reflected in our desires, needs, and beliefs. We start out simply enough. When we are young, the verities are indeed engraved in stone. The story of Moses at Sinai and the biblical image are not incidental, yet, sooner or later, we learn that even time-honored moral systems like the "Ten Commandments" can produce a tortured conscience that is not at all like the guilt of acknowledged wrong doing. The commandments read, "Honor thy father and mother," but they also read, "Do not bear false witness." What then shall we do if we must testify to the wrong doing of a father or mother? To be sure, we may work out new meanings for "honor" or "false witness." We can be quite inventive behind the cloak of eternal truths. Invention unadmitted, however, easily turns into sophistry. How then shall we judge when we cross that divide? The habits of childhood must flicker at such moments, and if we have been taught that rules are morality, the invitation to indifference, even cynicism, is not far behind.

We meet other moral ambiguities. Growing up is marked by the discovery that worthy goals run into each other. We want moral certainty but not at the price of integrity. We want success but not with the loss of decency. We want to protect our children from evil but not by keeping them childish. We want to avoid insulting our friends but not at the cost of truthfulness. Moral experience comes to feel like "a blooming buzzing confusion," to use William James's phrase.

We may admit this confusion, but we feel the loss of our moral anchor. We had learned that moral rules were fixed and secure. The early lessons stick with us, so we adopt strategies that hide us from this confusion and it from us. Basic to such strategies is the denial of the world as it is. We reduce it to manageable proportions. We invent little vices like "white lies" that are beneath moral notice, or offer big justifications like the "reason of state" that are beyond moral notice. Living by the rules is itself another way of achieving denial, and that is why our "well-behaved student" is a constant temptation.

We simplify life by retreating to the comforts of family and tribe. In the smaller world of readily shared symbols and known authorities, values are more accessible and more dependable. To be sure, the conflicts of intimacy are well documented in psychiatry, tribal warfare, and poetic tragedy. The tortured quality of intimacy is repressed or displaced, brought to consciousness only to vanish, yet the story of Cain and Abel is a tale of family values gone awry even if the root metaphor is cosmic, not intimate. The dramas of Sophocles are peopled by kings and queens, princes, priests, and generals, but it is the disarray of mothers and sons, fathers and daughters, brothers and sisters that creates the tragedy. However, for all the moral and emotional tensions of intimacy, it remains quite cozy. In the world of personal connections, even our hates are comfortable. In that world— where each of us began and which each of us recalls—we can announce unequivocally what is morally sound. Above all, the players of intimacy are known to us, even if we do not always like them.

The moral availability of intimacy is, to be sure, a useful fiction, and it helps us grow up. Unfortunately, intimacy itself is under threat today. The world out there always intruded to shape and reshape it, but today our world does so in ways that have deadly results. The unwanted and the unattached child is all too frequent. The family is changing as the "single-parent" family and the "two-career" family become ordinary, so even the wanted and loved child begins life in a less than secured intimacy today. The stabilities that initiated us, vanish though they must as we grow up, are decreasingly available even to the very young.[2] The experience of intimacy itself becomes problematic, and with it, the basis for moral development becomes even shakier than before.[3]

To be sure, the family always reflected the world out there, hence the agricultural patterns of Judaea in the Old Testament or the classical images of Sophoclean drama or, closer to home, the industrial portraits of Dickensian novels. The moral clarity of intimacy masks the impact of nature, society, and culture, and justifies their inescapable demands on conscience and consciousness.[4] Seeming to protect us against the moral confusions of the world, intimacy succeeds in hiding what goes on by letting us believe we can close our doors to the world. At the same time, that security is necessary even if fictional.

In today's world, the "island of sanity" hidden behind the doors of family and tribe grows smaller and smaller. Yes, protective isolation was always an illusion, but it got us going by giving us an initial confidence. Now we learn at an earlier and earlier age of the nearness of public events. Society shifts its attentions and we unavoidably are touched. In the 1950s, conformity was a moral problem, in the 1960s it was individuality; and the cycle repeats.[5] The issue that stirs us even when at home may be an overwhelming one like peace, loyalty, hunger, or population; these issues are felt personally although they are far away and out of control. The Chernobyl accident brings nuclear energy to consciousness in a new way; fear of AIDs introduces new anxieties into sexuality. The issues that invade intimacy may be less global, like the violence that erupts because Blacks are moving into a neighborhood or the dismay when a sports hero is caught taking drugs. However it happens, we bring the world into our homes as students, workers, or citizens. A walk through city streets on the way to school causes the child to carry the world into the classroom. The TV screen, the press, and the films inescapably expose us all, and for more and more of the time. Things don't stay in their compartments— they never did, but before we could act as if they did. Now very little holds still; at the same time we are more naked than ever, and we know it.

In turn, we take our intimacies into the school, office, and voting booth. A quarrel at home brings anger to work or classroom. Prejudice learned at "mother's knee" becomes principle in town meeting or at election time. That was ever so. Today, we are thrust into the public life sooner and with scarcely matured egos, and so a shrinking intimacy inflicts violence, anger, and hostility on a public life that is already hardly manageable and so much more crowded than ever before. The moral situation becomes more problematic just when the moral resources have grown more shaky.

Experience was always simultaneoulsy intimate and public, cozy and alien. Moral education always happened in an environment filled with differences, contrasts, and contradictions. Today, the environment has grown even more varied, confusing, and unstable. Whereas once moral habits could achieve a great deal, modern instabilities reduce their usefulness. When, as we must, we break through our strategies of denial, we are returned to Socratic ignorance in a new and poignant way, forced to confront the puzzles of the moral life just when wearied and disarmed.

We confront this fearful ambiguity with fewer "natural" resources. Facing this situation, we are likely to seek even more rigid simplicities. Hence a rampant fundamentalism appears everywhere in our time. Since it is less a matter of theological conviction than of psychological need, we may expect it to grow.

Complicating matters even more, industrial and postindustrial societies transfer moral education to institutions that were in the past only backups for intimacy—hence the fact of the overburdened school. However, we find out that our institutions do not defend us unless, like the Amish or the Hassidim, we choose to live in another reality. Client relationships are not friendships, and "support networks" are not families. Understandably then, we call even more loudly for a return to the values of family and church. We blame the school but cannot dismiss it. Ironically, the loving, unconflicted families and communities of the past are more myth than history, but that does not stop us either. Intimacy and its story put boundaries around us and we long for those boundaries, but they are vanishing. We know that we cannot "go home again" because the community of yesterday is no more.

II

Already difficult, moral education is made more difficult by sectarian warfare, and this is understandable as a search for security. The fact of moral ambiguity, however, does not dictate any one view of the world. Some of us are secularists who find their morals within nature and culture. Others are religionists who hold that moral authority is unambiguously fixed into the universe. That, of itself, does not make for fundamentalism or even dogmatism. It is thus wrong headed for secularists to dismiss a religious point of view even if, for too many, religion is only a defense against uncertainty or a political ploy. We need to recall, by way of correcting secularist stereotypes, the terrifying uncertainties of the "man of faith": "Lord I believe, help me in my unbelief," he cries. For the religionist, the unfinishable experience of moral truthfulness may be interpreted as the ignorance of the believer and not the inadequacy of the world. Thus, the religionist can call for moral education in language not unfamiliar to the secularist.[6]

The believer mistakes his opponent, too. He accuses the secularist of reducing all alternatives to relativism and all relativism to chaos, but when we are not tempted to make partisan moves, we know that to admit to unfinished business is not to opt for nihilism. After all, we rely on probabilities to guide the sciences and technologies, the policies and practices of modern life. Indeed, it might be argued that the successes of modernity rest on acknowledging the usefulness of grasped uncertainties. It is not wrong headed on the face of it then to look for the benefits of moral doubt either.

Over and over again, we struggle to recover the notion that multiple interpretations of similar experiences are possible and sensible. Respectfulness is thus an intellectually sound idea and not merely a sentiment of toleration, and, if we are to find usable answers to moral questions, we cannot afford the luxuries or securities of sectarianism. Tribal walls—liberal or conservative—are no longer tenable in a world so impacted and in a society so varied. Somehow, then, we must get beyond the temptation on all sides to put people apart. Moral education, since it must empower us to make judgements in a world we did not choose and among people we did not invite, must be inclusive or it will fail. In short, the search for moral education is also the search for a reconstructed public philosophy, for a recovered sense of the common good.

A sign that many of us really know this—although we do not know how to go about it—is the effort to dismiss our differences for the sake of a set of "core" values.[7] That search, which appears over and over again, is only partially successful. Civic values, common courtesies, and usable conventions are indeed available, nor should their importance be minimized. At the same time, such "core" values must avoid conflict or else they would quickly cease to be acceptable. Hence, they suffer from deliberate ambiguity or intended superficiality.

For example, loyalty and patriotism seem self-evidently good. For the sake of sociability, however, we are not allowed to ask whether or not our society deserves our loyalty, whether it serves the common good. Nonetheless, few of us would be prepared to accept the burden of Josiah Royce's "loyalty to loyalty" or to take our patriotism the way Socrates took his sense of the city of Athens:

Imagine that I am about to play truant . . . and [that] the laws and the government come and interrogate me: "Tell us, Socrates . . . are you going by an act of yours to overturn us. . . ? Do you imagine that a state can subsist and not be overthrown in which decisions of law have no power but are set aside and trampled upon by individuals?". . . "Well then since you were brought into the world and nurtured and educated by us, can you deny . . . that you are our child and slave, as your fathers were before you?"[8]

Thus, unfortunately, "core" values fail us just when we need them, just when we must make them clear and unequivocal.

III

Modernist and traditionalist, liberal and conservative, absolutist and sceptic—none of us entered the moral situation as a "blank tablet." Consequently, we might look again at intimacy, but this time from within our own development. We all learned our moral values at home first, so when home and household are threatened, moral education is deeply problematic. Nonetheless, no matter how threatened, that is still where we began. Later, our friends taught us; the "street" taught us; radio, press, and TV taught us. At the same time, we never simply echoed anyone else—not even our parents in the most stable of families. To be sure, we were not strikingly original. It was a matter of small departures. Rarely did any of us, like Abraham, break the idols of the tribe. Things accrued for us. Only after the fact, just when we were losing their security, did we find our morals in neat categories. We muddled through, now helped and now puzzled by what we learned.

We also learned how to converse morally. We learned how to play moral language games partly in self-protection. In the common school or the changing neighborhood, those games crossed the boundaries of other people's games, and this led us to still newer games. Thus, for example, we played tolerance games, pluralism games, and civics games. Nevertheless, the moral games deepest in us retained a special insider feature.

Frequently we developed treaty habits for the sake of social survival, but we did not surround those treaties with moral sanctity. In other words, we learned how to get along—treating our own game as sacred, the others as conventional. As we say in social situations, "Let's not discuss religion or politics." Of course, on special occasions like religious or patriotic holidays, the games were transformed and the community boundaries expanded temporarily. Thus a Jewish mayor marched on St. Patrick's Day and the momentarily Irish crowd applauded. The habits that the games taught us were convenient. If they had a moral content at all, we did not separate it out. Our moral education came to us mixed up with lessons of politeness, conventionality, and legality. Most of us still have trouble separating moral questions from those of law and courtesy.

As we grew up—and today we grow up very quickly—events forced us to apply what we had learned in situations that never quite fit with what we were told. Still, we were not ready to depart the past. For some, this incoherence of past and present was read as a failure of moral insight; for others it was moral development, but that is interpretation—the common experience was that things didn't fit.

Meanwhile, moral fashions changed the ways in which moral ideas were conveyed, and we learned these too. New languages appeared, for example, the language of equality and justice came to be shaped by notions like "affirmative action" even as it in turn was legitimated by claims of justice, and we found ourselves learning strange and difficult things at an earlier age. Nine- and ten-year-olds, for example, were discussing "surrogate motherhood" in a classroom I visited last year. Catechism was replaced by discussion group; preaching changed as it moved from pulpit to mass media. The liberal, after the orgy of the 1960s or the Freudianism of the 1920s, rediscovered moral categories and began to give up the temptation to reduce ethics to therapy.

We went to school and the ranges of intimacy grew wider, and opened up toward a public life. In schools, more than anywhere else, our moral biographies came to reflect intellectual fashion, too. Moral history attended to this or that moral priority, and that shaped what happened to us in school. Caught up in the busyness of teaching and learning, most teachers—much less students—did not understand classroom moves as a matter of mood or style, or a shift in attention.

Instead, we became, without knowing it, liberals or conservatives, religious or secular, defenders of this or that virtue. We claimed that the way we found things out came first, as in the arguments about authority or intuition, or we became partisans of substantive values like justice, love, or integrity. Thus the 1960s elevated "gut feeling" and the 1980s called for a return to the virtues—and neither students nor teachers confessed their partiality. We were unwitting patriots of our causes. The school had not taught us the blessings of Socratic ignorance at all.

In classrooms, our language was more elaborate than its meaning warranted. We learned to engage in complex games—social and political games, and not only language games—whose outcomes were known in advance. However, neither we nor those who looked at us from the outside understood that we were undergoing the exercises of development. "Practical" people were everywhere, and they derided schooling while being blindly partisan of "the bottom line." Of course, this was only their unexamined value, but neither they nor we realized it, so we accepted values like "productivity" and "accountability." We heard their voices in the academy, the media, and even at home, and learned to suspect schooling at the same time that we were enjoying it. We grew impatient with the classroom because we were told by the world outside that we already knew what moral reality was, but we were also inveterate puzzle makers and solvers. so when we were allowed to go directly to an outcome—given the answers, so to speak—we were disappointed without knowing why. Then we wondered at the aridity of the classroom and complained about our teachers and fellow students.

Moral crusades affected us too. We learned to take offense, or to feel alienated. Some of us resisted the short cuts—practical or moral—not because we disagreed but because we felt put upon. We wanted the pleasure of working it out for ourselves, even of exploring dead ends and circuitous byways. Hence, the value and ubiquity of the college "bull session" and the high school debate, and the deadlines of things like compulsory chapel.

Although we can only recall bits of moral biography—and it was ever thus—we recognize the play of attentiveness, mood, and termperament in them. We know that when and where we went to school had much to do with how we were schooled. This could help us to avoid useless argument with those who want to proclaim this or that virtue, or with those who advocate this or that skill, like moral reasoning, but we didn't learn very much about stepping back. "Choosing up sides," which we did learn, is a temptation we seldom resist.

A penchant for exclusive choices misleads us. The record of moral advocacy is ample on the point, yet moral wisdom is always in the process of give and get, and always the process itself is a moral problem. A paradigm is Plato's *Euthyphro*. Socrates remarks,

But friend Euthyphro, if that which is holy is the same with that which is dear to God, and is loved because it is holy, then that which is dear to God would have been loved as being dear to God; but if that which is dear to God is dear to him because loved by him, then that which is holy would have been holy because loved by him. . . . For one is of a kind to be loved because it is loved and the other is loved because it is of a kind to be loved.[9]

The dialogue reveals the question of method—"because it is loved of the gods"—and substance—"because it is of a kind to be loved by the gods." It introduces us to a perennial moral issue, the relationship of "is" and "ought," as in the distinction between the loved and the lovable. It points out the tension between religious certainty and pedagogical scepticism, and it exhibits the spiral pattern of departure and return, the "same" question renewed, that is a permanent feature of moral history.

Socrates expects Euthyphro to resist, indeed invites it. The lack of an ending is typical of education, and is troubling too, so liberals ignore Socrates and try to pretend that there are "neutral" skills that are applicable indifferently to any subject matter, and conservatives claim the self-evidence of a moral common sense. We hear talk of "civil religion" or the Judaeo-Christian heritage.[10] Unfortunately, too many on all sides are willing to turn the classroom into a pulpit. Affronted when we do not agree, they lose sight of the difference between school and church, between classroom and party.

How we learn and what we teach are rooted in different views of the world and the person, but these, whatever form they take, begin and end as metaphor. If it is the self-seeking individual, our psychology is one thing; if it is altruism, then it is another, yet we try to prove one or the other, as if metaphor were demonstrable instead of being enlightening, appropriate, and useful. To do justice to the complexities of moral biography, we need to be schooled in comparative anthropologies, psychologies, and philosophies. We need to be morally literate and critical, but that hasn't happened.

At times, we teach virtue as we teach science or mathematics. We look for a cumulative content, working out more and more "advanced" moral lessons. At other times, an ideal drives our ethics as in Machiavelli's passionate search for Italy and peace. At still other times, we try to organize our subject in axiomatic form—into principles, rules, and applications—as Spinoza did in his *Ethics.* Of course, the more interesting issues of that text escape into the footnotes and commentaries, while the axioms, postulates, and definitions stand there like an unfleshed skeleton.

Misled by our need for stability and by the fashion that attends to morals, we achieve a "discipline" called "ethics" only to find it outdated just as it is completed. Like military strategists, we fight today's wars with yesterday's tactics. Thus the graded lessons of the nineteenth-century schoolroom were turned irrelevant by the move from countryside to city even as the readers and primers were being published, and Spinoza's *Ethics* "ordine geometrico demonstrate" was outdated by a nascent seventeenth-century empiricism even as it was being circulated. The story of moral fashion and intellectual theme is a cautionary tale of dependabilities that go awry over and over again. Moral biography is thus shaped by the securities of intimacy and by their disappearance.

Perhaps the most dramatic examples of this quicksand pattern are to be found in the dilemmas of biomedical ethics as we try to figure out who shall live and who shall die. We face a deepening puzzlement about what is and what is not alive, and an even deeper anxiety because human beings must decide such matters.

Experience continues to escape moral fashion. The securities of tradition do not avoid the quicksand either. The reverent echo of the wisdom of the fathers is no mere repetition. Moral commentary, in conservative and liberal institutions alike, is a lesson in reconstruction which is, however, often masked to avoid accusations of heresy. Bible stories are told and retold, but the differences in the telling are unavoidably present in the teller. Canon law needs its interpreters, and Torah requires Talmud. Even literalists use the English of James and not the Aramaic, Hebrew, or Greek of the fathers.

Liberals cannot take comfort from their liberalism either. Moral history does not insure that the latest is always the most truthful. Even the moral radical builds on yesterday. Modernists in any age— and the warfare between the ancients and the moderns is itself part of our tradition—are caught responding to novelty in experience already past. Finally, both traditionalist and modernist need to equip students for the unforeseeable, and both find themselves chasing a situation that is always just beyond reach. Above all, this calls for a confession of inadequacy on all sides, so again we come back to the Socratic paradox: "I know that I know nothing."

IV

We enter in the middle of things, looking to remembered intimacies for stability and trying to hold the situation still long enough to learn how to encounter it intelligently. Here and there a suggestion for doing so is made. Today, given a scientific metaphor, we try to separate inquiry with its alleged objectivity from commitment with its aura of passion, but ideas and feelings, structures and histories are caught in each other. We cannot "think critically," "clarify values," or "solve moral dilemmas" in general.[11] We choose examples, anecdotes, and stories to work with, and when we choose, we reveal our values. For example, Harvard's Lawrence Kohlberg used the "Heinz" dilemma to test for "stages" of moral development. Presented as a conflict between property rights and lifesaving values—shall the husband steal or not steal the life-preserving drug in order to save his wife's life?—it poses alternative meanings of the social contract. Without contractual language, however, the dilemma itself would cease to exist. "Values clarification" assumes the priority of toleration. Those who, more traditionally, opt for virtue, reveal their temperament by what is first, what is last, and what is omitted. No one is above the battle.

Frustrated by the elusiveness of moral education and wearied of a struggle that has no end, we are tempted by formula, and hence the fads and illusions that afflict our subject. The fad must fall out of favor, however. We then fall back on the reproduction in our children of the values with which we are comfortable even when we know that our children are not ourselves. We are all afflicted by this fundamentalist temptation, and that is why it never disappears. At the same time, we have a romance with the science. Thus even the fundamentalist tries, unsuccessfully, to turn Bible stories into "creation science." Others try, as unsuccessfully, to turn morality into a quantitative discipline. Like modern Utilitarians, they seek to measure the "greatest good for the greatest number," but then they do battle

over the weights to be given to the various "goods."[12] Unacknowl-
edged metaphors frustrate us because they really lead us to different
facts. The partisans grow defensive or angry or, finally, indifferent.
Warfare comes to characterize the alternatives, and instead of trying
to make sense of moral experience, we do battle.

There is no escape, however, from our moral expectations. Moral
education is rooted in personal need and the urgency of personal
decision. This existential realization is, to be sure, frightening. It
introduces individuality where we desperately want to be settled
and secure in some kind of collectivity. Blind to notions of metaphor
and temperament, worried by the uncertainties of experience, the
modernist opts for ethical thinking that is analytic and deliberately
antihistorical, nor is it surprising that in response, intuitive and neo-
traditionalist moves should appear.[13] Unfortunately, neither satisfies.

Theorists have moral biographies too, so their defenses take shape
in a special way as they become enamored with abstraction, which is
at the center of their biographies. The appearance of a scientific style
in modern ethical thought is itself a function of our moment in history. It is characterized among other things by a deep separation between ethical knowing and moral practice. Rarely then does moral
action benefit from the academy. Consultants, to be sure, are abundant. A scandal in politics, law, or business stirs us, perhaps, to insert
a "course in ethics" into the professional curriculum or to adopt a
professional "code." The ongoing presence of moral thinking in the
marketplace is, however, hard to find. Economics, following an early
modern mythology about the neutrality of the sciences, is taken to
be morally indifferent. Politics is driven by an allegedly neutral realism. For social anthropology, the world is value-free and morality a
cultural artifact to be described. In daily life, however, the world is
morally laden although language and convention may serve more to
conceal than reveal. Consequently, "realism" is itself a moral preference,[14] and laissez-faire is the consequence of a moral judgement on
how best to achieve the common good.[15]

V

Before looking at the reconstruction of school and classroom, yet
one more puzzle is stirred by the question, "Can virtue be taught?"
The subject matter itself is problematic, which is why we move back

and forth between the substance of ethics and the ways we acquire it. Argument about the nature and content of morality or the appropriate role of ethical thinking continues. We are hardly nearer agreement on ethics now than we were 2,500 years ago. Platonists, who embed values in the "heaven beyond the heavens," still confront sceptics who deny the objectivity of moral values. Utilitarians judge morality by the consequences of human action. Kantians maintain that the moral law inheres in a special moral reality. The debate between partisans of the "good" and partisans of the "right" continues. The former look to purposes, the latter to processes. Some give priority to welfare, others to fairness. Intuitionists "know" the good directly; rationalists construct axiomatic systems; conventionalists describe moral "rules of the road." Naturalists connect the "is" and the "ought," seeking to build a bridge between ethics and moral psychology, between the desirable and the desired. Positivists condemn the connection as the "naturalistic fallacy." Little wonder then that the academy is dismissed from the arena of life judgements as pointless.

Day-to-day moral decisions, however, are no less conflicted. Were we really secure in our ordinary values, we might with relief leave the philosophers to their arguments, but in moral experience too, as we well know, there is less and less agreement as our world grows larger. Advocates are to be found on the many sides of any morally interesting question. In the press, from the pulpit, in the legislatures, we debate a familiar agenda without expecting resolution—abortion, surrogate motherhood, euthenasia, capital punishment, and so on, and the situation promises to become more and not less difficult as matters of life and death become questions of choice, not fate. Decisions about war and peace or in biomedical ethics produce new complexities for which we are unprepared. The massive and poorly understood drive to organize everything and everywhere of modern corporate societies leaves us puzzled about moral obligation. Despite a growing literature, there is scant wisdom on the "moral responsibility of business" or the moral obligations of government, yet life and death, war and peace, power and influence are unavoidably presented in our daily lives. Little wonder then that moral anxiety is a feature of contemporary biography. Little wonder, too, that the pressure for moral education increases almost in direct relationship to the increase of our moral confusion.

At the same time, ethical analysis and moral history do help us find usable notions, for example, that moral judgement requires a

certain "distance" from self-interest; that moral imperatives require
an assessment of the possible and the impossible or, as the philosopher puts it, "ought implies can"; that moral variety recommends a
certain toleration; that moral novelty advises the need for dependable methods of moral inquiry. To be sure, none of these ideas is ever
secured. For example, the egoist may take "self-interest" to be the
criterion of moral judgement and think thereby to deny the possibility of moral objectivity, but the ethical egoist must still deal with
the moral equality of all egos and the problem of the "free rider,"
that is, the distinctions between self-interest, selfishness, and opportunism, these distinctions are never only a "matter of taste."

It is clear enough to all but the extremist among us that no single
method of moral inquiry and no completed moral code is available
or is likely to be in the future. Given the essential "fuzziness" of
moral biography, no single moral pedagogy will serve either. Like
it or not, moral conflict will not be settled in our time any more than
it was in the past, and even the extremists know they cannot have
their way without oppressing the "enemy" and inviting perpetual
warfare.

We cannot establish moral education by exclusive attention to
common-sense morality either, because common sense fails us just
where we are most in need. We are creatures too of our passions as
much as of our reasons. Interesting moral questions are felt as well as
argued. A strain of the arbitrary persists in all serious moral discourse.
The struggles between secular and religiously based morality, between
left and right, between individualist and communalist, take place
inside and outside of the walls of school and academy, and are inevitably shaped by our deepest feelings.

The outcome, too often, is to convert pluralism into separatism,
and toleration into a treaty relationship between alien parties. On
this dubious ground, we succeeded for a long time in developing
common schooling that satisfied the expectations of most people
most of the time. Political peace, however, was achieved at the cost
of moral imperialism and, more recently, of moral superficiality.
Furthermore, the unspoken assumptions that grounded that peace
have vanished.[16] New players with newly found powers have entered
the game. Schools have again become a battleground, and even a pre-
tended moral neutrality does not defend them from attack. Church–
state issues, which are a measure of social conflict and not simply of
religious differences, arise more and more frequently. Evolution,

creationism, Bible reading, sexuality, prayer, censorship, and patriotism become points of controversy.

In this complicated situation, some of us will continue to insist that our own answers and only our own answers are acceptable whether in school, home, or society. If this sense of things prevails, then warfare or an uneasy peace are the only alternatives; but then, society itself is at risk. What shall we do and where shall we turn if that risk is unacceptable and moral neutrality an illusion? We began with the Socratic question, "Can virtue be taught?" We answered with Socratic ignorance. However, that is an invitation to moral education and not a denial of its possibility. Ignorance is the stimulus and schooling the response, but what kind of schooling?

Notes

1. Erich Fromm uses this striking phrase in his discussion of the dynamics of fascism. See *Escape from Freedom* (New York: Rhinehart and Co., 1941).

2. See, for example, Daniel Patrick Moynihan, *Family and Nation* (New York: Harcourt Brace and Jovanovich, 1986); also Karl Zinsmeister, "Family's Tie to the American Dream," *Public Opinion* 9 (September–October 1986: 3-6; and Harold Howe II, "The Prospect for Children in the United States," *Phi Delta Kappan* 68 (November 1986): 191-96.

3. For example, David Elkind reminds us of alternative metaphors for the family in *The Hurried Child* (Reading, Mass.: Addison-Wesley, 1981):

Just as children have traditionally been seen as "plants" that "unfold from within" or as "raw material" that has to be "shaped from without," families have also been looked upon in metaphoric terms. One view of the family is that of a "haven in a heartless world," a sort of refuge from the trials and tribulations of the competitive world. . . . A second contrary image of the family is that it is not so much a refuge as a "prison" that promotes the worst rather than the best in its inmates. . . . [I]n socialist and authoritarian countries, the family is often seen as the enemy of the state and communal child-rearing is a way of lessening its debilitating effects. . . . At one time or another American families have been attacked for "momism," for "permissiveness," or for putting children into "double binds" (for example, the mother who says, "Come and give me a kiss," but whose body language says that she finds the child offensive). (p. 81)

4. See, for example, Sigmund Freud's *Civilization and Its Discontents*, trans. and ed. James Strachey (New York and London: Norton, 1961).

5. It is interesting to compare today's language with yesterday's. For example, two popular themes of the 1960s were "de-schooling society" (see Ivan Illich, *De-Schooling Society*, New York: Harper and Row, 1970) and "education as a

subversive activity." Today, we are more likely to find reference to "basics," "excellence," "discipline," and even to "re-schooling society."

6. One recent example: Sister Mary Peter Traviss, OP, *Student Moral Development in the Catholic School*, NCEA Keynote Series (Washington, D.C.: National Catholic Education Association, 1985).

7. A typical recent report was headlined, "Consensus Is Sought on Instilling Moral Values" and reported a keynote address by Martin E. Marty at a conference, "Education and Religion in a Multireligious Society," held at George Washington University, Washington, D.C., during the week of April 29, 1987. Professor Marty called on various religious communities to agree on what values should be taught and noted that all religions are based on similar moral codes. Kirsten Goldberg, "Consensus is Sought on Instilling Moral Values," *Education Week* (May 6, 1987): 9.

8. Plato, "Crito," in *The Dialogues of Plato*, vol. 1, translated by Benjamin Jowett (New York: Random House, 1937), pp. 434–435.

9. Plato, "Euthyphro," in *The Dialogues of Plato*, vol. 1, trans. B. Jowett, p. 392.

10. For example, see Robert N. Bellah et al., *Habits of the Heart* (New York: Harper and Row, 1985).

11. Moral reasoning, critical thinking, values clarification, philosophy for children, and dilemma discussions are among the major pedagogies of today's moral education.

12. Utilitarianism is probably most familiar to us by way of the slogan, "The greatest good for the greatest number." The notion of calculating "goods" appears in the nineteenth-century work of Jeremy Bentham, James Mill, and John Stuart Mill. A reading of John Stuart Mill's essay, *Utilitarianism*, is still rewarding. Naturally, much more complex and technical work has been done since then in the development of guides to social and economic policy.

13. For example, see Alasdair MacIntyre, *After Virtue* (South Bend, Indiana: University of Notre Dame Press, 1981).

14. A reading of Macchiavelli's *The Prince*, particularly chapters 15–21, reveals the moral underpinnings of so-called political "realism."

15. Adam Smith in *The Wealth of Nations* draws upon his philosophy of "moral sentiments" and describes the workings of the well-known "invisible hand." Clearly, for Smith, the moral end of the public welfare justifies the operations of a free market, or, as Bernard Mandeville put it, "Private Vices, Public Virtues."

16. One revealing index of the disappearance of a "Protestant" consensus can be found in the church–state cases brought to the U.S. Supreme Court. For example, in the first decades after the end of World War II, a group of cases concerned themselves with "released time," the provision of public moneys to parochial schools, prayer and bible reading, for example, Everson *v.* Board of Education (1947), McCollum *v.* Board of Education (1948), Doremus *v.* Board

of Education (1952), Zorach *v.* Clauson (1952), Engel *v.* Vitale (1962), Abington *v.* Schemp (1963), and Murray *v.* Curlett (1963). Since the beginning of Ronald Reagan's second presidential term in 1984, a number of major cases have reached the high court, giving further evidence that the quarrel continues; for example, in June of 1985, four major church–state decisions were handed down concerning silent prayer in public schools, the right to have a day off on the sabbath, and the sending of public school teachers into parochial schools. We may expect more of the same.

3

Taking the Middle Ground:
Of Schools and Schooling

I

When we add up the hours, days, and years we spend in school, we can understand that it, after the home, is the place where children build a second biography. Adults, too, go to school. They attend workshops, courses, and training programs. We may not be an educated society, but we are surely a school-going one. To be sure, the children of the underclass are more likely to be schooled by the streets and only to serve time in school. Moral education, however, needs to meet them too, but that is another project.[1] For many children, school days are extended by nursery programs, after-school programs, and summer programs. At the same time, we complain that we do not spend enough time with "hard" subjects, and we compare ourselves unfavorably to the Europeans or the Japanese. However, that has more to do with nationalist and economic competition and less with educational values.

Never again, except in the workplace, will we give so much time and energy to a single activity, but unlike the workplace, most schooling happens when we are growing up. It is, therefore, unsurprising that in the process our values will also be formed. Moral education is an inevitable subject matter. We catch and catch onto what society and culture take to be important and trivial. We also catch onto how we're supposed to talk about such things, and, finally, we catch onto the gaps between talk and conduct.

Our teachers, like our parents, are interested in our growth. We develop relationships with them—and they with us—in a setting that

37

is supportive as family is supportive. We will, by and large, be protected by them in our errors and encouraged by them to risk the bounds of conduct without paying the ultimate penalties.

To be sure, schooling will have another face, too. Love and distance will compete. The school will look very much like the rest of society, not least of all like the workplace. Economic benefits will justify both. This was the way of farm and apprenticeship in an earlier time: function mixed with personal relationships. Today, the school gives the message of a different kind of workplace, not least of all by its factory-like organization and appearance. Its architecture is not neutral; rules, time clocks, and measurements surround us. We feel the shift away from intimacy and toward impersonality. At some point in our school years, the school as a community vanishes, although the rhetoric of community is preserved.

The image of school as workplace conveys values, often unintended values. We are sincere when we talk of caring, growth, and learning. At the same time, we are concerned with performance and with meeting external standards. We are dedicated to outcomes as much as to development. An open admission of this conjunction of school values and industrial production is hard to come by, for we do not want to believe that schooling is really a way of doing social and economic allocation. We try to separate schooling from work-life, from the alienations of caste and class, in our hopes if not in our practices. We aim for the democratic school but have a hard time achieving it.

To be sure, schooling everywhere reflects its culture and prepares the young for admission to society. In that, we are by no means unusual, but schools have also been at the edge of society and culture, at the point where replication and criticism join. That, for example, and not job protection, was the intent of academic freedom and intellectual autonomy, but independence is less and less likely today.[2] Schooling, in other words, has a moral and political assignment: to serve both as a reminder of generative ideals and as a source of their reconstruction. This explains the traditional conflict between "town and gown" and the perennial suspicion of schools as "hotbeds" of radicalism.[3] In an industrial and corporate society, however, we are more likely to reflect Durkheim's notion that schooling aims for "discipline," the willing acceptance of the norms of collective life.[4] This transformation of schooling into industrial instruction generates the moral education we have and makes problematic the task of achieving the moral education we need.

II

Whenever we are deliberately helped to learn, we are in school. We experience it, however, as an interruption of social activity. We step to one side in order to learn before we return from school to use what we have found. At the same time, schooling is an activity in itself and has its own outcomes and pleasures. We realize our powers, solve problems, and answer questions. Not least of the rewards is a common life with other students. While schooling may begin with transmitting information or training for skills, it also sidesteps the merely present and the merely practical. Memory and imagination acquire tangibility as we come to know our fellow members' pasts, presents, and futures in literature, song, and story. If we ignore its historical reality, schooling is short-circuited. In other words, schooling is not only functional. It is found in personal learning and explorations.

Moral experience, like all experience, is unfinished. Whether we are liberal or conservative, we are called on to make judgements in unexpected situations and to talk about these with others. There is then a natural fit between schooling and moral education. We miss out on that connection, on the one side, by thinking that schooling can be morally neutral and, on the other, by thinking that "morals" are really the business of family and church. Both sides reflect a confusion between our needs and those of the relatively uncluttered tribal society where the public and the intimate were intertwined.

Although schooling takes place in a "public" space, it is not thereby a "state" agency. That confuses source of support with identity, and elevates social function to the point of idolatry. A similar confusion on the left reduces schooling to class interests because of this functionalism. In fact, schooling is neither as intimate as the family nor as public as the state; it is somewhere in between. Schooling occupies a middle ground epistemologically and institutionally, so we should expect to find that schools are always embattled when they are doing their work. It is a sign of failure when schools cease to stir up an argument.

Schooling is located between parties that contend for the intelligence and loyalty of the young, for their "souls" one might say, yet it is not a party to that battle. Its students come and go, and do not make their home permanently in school. It is therefore the natural locus for relationships that are intimate and open, private and public, personal and social. It is mistaken, therefore, to think that schools in moral matters are agencies of last resort expected to do the moral work of person and culture only because others have failed, yet we ought not to be surprised at the combination of nostalgia and politics found in reference back to family and church. Moral education, well done, is powerfully corrosive of the accepted. At the same time, those of us who live in schools reflect that same nostalgia. So, except for schools with an announced moral "mission" like Roman Catholic schools, we are defensive about doing the work of moral education; we resent it as an imposition and are resented as intruders. Nonetheless, when schooling is viewed as the middle ground in a culture that radically redefines the public and the intimate, we begin to understand why it must attend to moral education just as it attends to history, art, science, mathematics, or physical education. The stuff of our subject matter is neither purely personal nor entirely social.

Indeed, when we look at what really happens in schools, we realize that the moral life of students is dealt with in many different ways. Tasks are shared, truthfulness is valued, growth is respected, equality of participation is encouraged. However, because of the ambivalence with which we approach moral education and because of the resistance of other institutions, the development of the nascent strengths of schooling is seldom realized. Moral consciousness is neglected and implicit messages left uncriticized.

As with all schooling, moral education begins with an interruption. We hesitate. In face of our impulse to moral certainty, this hesitation is threatening. Schooling, therefore, is always suspect. Again, our memories are helpful. We recall the frequency with which moral conflicts arose as we grew up. We didn't know what to do but we knew we had to do something, whether arguing with our parents, lying to a friend, struggling with sexuality, or what have you. If we were lucky, our teachers allowed us, safely, to expose our moral doubts. In school, we could enjoy the support of a community without risking the sanctions of the judging parent or the punishing society. We could "be bad" without feeling the guilt of betraying love or loyalty. That is why the misbehaving student was so often a figure of fun and why the loss of good humor in schools today is both symptom and problem of the loss of schooling. In fact, our teachers invited our puzzles and our doubts, and seemed almost perversely to enjoy them. Thus, just as teachers use error to generate learning, so the moral teacher uses doubt to stir moral development.

The doubts that initiate learning are felt and are not simply an abstract puzzle. In schools such feelings can be introduced deliberately, self-consciously. We need not wait for them to happen. Schooling is intentional. Effective schooling converts the intentional into the existential, and not just for students. Consider, by way of example, the following note sent by a school principal to his faculty on opening day. Those of us who work in school know the overwhelming detail on those first days—the press of the mundane tasks like finding one's room in a new school, getting chalk and erasers and paper and pencil, learning the regulations—so it seems uncharitable to interrupt. Nonetheless, he writes:

Dear Teacher:

I am a survivor of a concentration camp. My eyes saw what no man should witness: gas chambers built by learned engineers; children poisoned by educated physicians; infants killed by trained nurses; women and babies shot and burned by high school and college graduates. So I am suspicious of education.

My request is: help your students become human. Your efforts must never produce learned monsters, skilled psychopaths, educated Eichmanns. Reading, writing, arithmetic are important only if they serve to make our children more human.[5]

Schooling expects us to interrupt everywhere. We break into the routines with constructed intrusions. We call attention. Intrusion is legitimate; it is also annoying. Along with the interruptions, we look for connections and reconnections between humanistic learning and humane conduct. At the same time, we don't want to be bothered; we have more important things to do. However, this helps us realize how easily we ignore interruptions and how tenuous those connections are. We can understand our students in ourselves. "Educated Eichmanns" are, as we know to our sorrow, not impossible. Their birth is in the use of detail to mask reality, in impatience for the sake of efficiency. Interruptions then will have to recur, to be insisted on, in order to break the reign of the banal. When, however, we view the school through the lens of function and efficiency, we separate schools from schooling. The so-called moral failures of our schools are rooted in this misguided functionalism, but they are also rooted in frustrated expectations: even our best efforts do not insure a morally best outcome.

Schooling stands apart from the ongoing life of persons. At the same time, schooling is a second biography for each of us. We develop friendships, languages, and rhythms that often begin and end with the school day, the school year. As we grow older, the separation between school life, work-life, and personal life increases. The young child in a "neighborhood school" studies and plays within the same community. The graduate student carries a skill or competence from place to place. The back-and-forth connections between our lives, unfortunately, are never easy, so the relationships of learning and doing are themselves a problem of schooling; nor is this solved by the progressive notion of "learning by doing," for "doing" under such conditions is itself a construction, a lesson. The progressive insight surely makes for a more adequate schooling, but its reference is still to the second biography.

Criticism of our schools cannot, therefore, be dismissed only as the posturing of left- or right-wing partisans. It arises from a misunderstanding of the middle ground and of the limits and possibilities of the second biography. We are frustrated with the wrong things: low test scores, teenage moral relativism, and the like. This alerts us to the fact that we have not learned about learning or else that we are fearful of learning. Common sense confuses schooling with training and then connects it to outcomes that can be measured, or as we say, using a business metaphor, "assessed." Even those who know better fall into this confusion. For example, former Secretary of Education William Bennett writes,

Teachers and principals must be willing to articulate character-building ideals and convictions to students. . . . Nor am I talking about moralizing. . . . We must have teachers and principals who not only state the difference between right and wrong but who make a real effort to live that difference in front of students . . . [and] we don't have to reinvent the wheel. . . . We already have . . . material that virtually all schools once taught to students for the sake of shaping character. . . . There is a very broad and very deep consensus out there on how to do this, and we fail in our duty if we fail to do so.[6]

To this statement we might reply as one education reporter did:

From the vantage point of the nation's capitol, character education must be understood as a political phenomenon—not a curricular or even an educational issue. . . . In speeches by President Reagan and those lower down in the ranks of the Administration, we are told that the major failure of our schools centers on the lack of instruction in values. Gary Bauer, formerly undersecretary of education and now domestic policy advisor at the White House, enunciated this theme in typical Administration fashion. "The problems of alcoholism, drug abuse, vandalism, promiscuity, and simple lack of common decency that pervade our schools," Bauer said, "are clearly related to the terrible state of moral education in the American classroom."[7]

At the same time, the debate reflects genuine concerns. The connections between knowing and doing are often indirect and never secured. We have added special features to this natural difficulty. Caught in the dilemmas of democratic pluralism and in love with the metaphor of value-neutral sciences, we have tried unsuccessfully to sever the connection between moral knowing and doing while insisting on it everywhere else. Thus in the worlds of business, technology, and government, we teach for utility as well as enjoyment. The study of history, English, science, or mathematics also leads to practice as historian, researcher, or scholar, and to applications in daily life as well, but we try to make schooling ideologically barren and consequently morally impractical. Thus we give credibility to the notion that schools are morally indifferent. We think we can set morality apart in some private world that schooling does not touch. This can only be mystifying. No small part of the resentment of schooling by its critics is the fruit of a lie that we come to believe: that by limiting itself to knowledge and skills or, on the conservative side, to so-called "basics," schooling can evade moral controversy. Resentment appears among teachers, too, who know that neither they nor their classrooms are morally insensitive or morally indifferent. The things we teach in schools and the ways we teach them are unavoidably caught in the moral situation. Finally, our students are not fools. They catch on to our evasions too and so, as it were, turn their backs on schools and schooling.

A destructive fiction haunts the present. At the same time, our pluralist society is growing more conscious of its pluralism and more respectful of personal, ethical, and religious variety. The same forces that stir social conflict and lead to war, riot, and terror are potentially materials of enrichment. While a generalized Protestant religiosity— "Kulturprotestantismus," as sociologist Peter Berger called it—persisted in our country, the tension of pluralism could be submerged except for rare outbreaks by offended minorities. That consensus impoverished schooling by narrowing moral choice and ignoring cultural richness as much as it violated personality, but we didn't catch on to the fact that it did. The call for a return to unquestioned core values is a reprise of that violation. However, the "good old days" were not necessarily good at all.

That Protestant common sense that lasted until World War II is gone, although not without a struggle.[8] Schools now confront diversity with all its ambiguity and conflict. When brought to awareness, diversity is essential to good schooling. That is why the modern school for all of its flaws is richer and more fascinating than schools of a century or even a few decades ago. We have "discovered" women, Blacks, Chicanos, native Americans; a globe that extends beyond England, Greece, or Rome, and other discoveries are still to be made. That is why the "3 R's," even when a "4th R" of religion is added, are a poor excuse for schooling. A token of the change going on is the concern for moral education itself. In an earlier day, it was simply subsumed under the rubric of ideological piety—or what was also called good character. The school was simply meant to echo church and family. The middle ground was to be morally boring.

Schools, at their best, have always been centers of conflict. When we have failed to appreciate the uses of conflict, however, we have impoverished the middle ground. Socrates, after all, was condemned for corrupting the young, St. Thomas for heresy, Dewey for radicalism. That tradition continues. Today, a "moral majority" complains that a "secular humanist conspiracy" has captured the schools, causing them to teach evolution and internationalism and neglect God and prayer. At the same time, both liberal and libertarian struggle for the independence of schooling in the face of an evolving statism. This confusing situation will, no doubt, become even more difficult in our pluriform society. The school is no longer emergent, as it once was, from family or church, which might laugh at it or criticize it but which also protected it. Conflict then announces that schooling is richer and riskier than before. As an institution among institutions, schools are also benevolently suppressed by the attractions of organization and rationalization.

With unintended irony, we delegate to schools activities that are value-laden, such as those in health care, early childhood development, after-school protection, and the maturation of interpersonal relationships including sexuality. Thus, we make a doubly illegitimate demand of schools: that they be morally neutral where they cannot be and that they take on nurturing roles reserved in more traditional societies to family and church. The burdened school—which is thereby forced to compromise schooling—is the symptom of an irresponsible society, one that has failed to reconstruct traditional institutions but has instead dumped its problems into convenient places.

To make this move acceptable, we disguise this shift of roles to the schools with the language of technocracy. As we hear so often, the school is available. With this abdication, we transfer the work of communal supports and services to schools, thereby acknowledging that traditional forms are emptied of their activity. Traditional institutions as a result resent the school and try to invade it even more. To normal threats stirred up by the critical activity of schooling is now added a territorial threat as well. Along the way, the school buries schooling in a morass of useful but distracting activities. It loses its way, missing the middle ground.

School organization becomes disjointed, overly bureaucratic, trapped into illusions of efficiency. Even when a school sets out to "teach values," it looks, typically, to another technology. That is why behavioral proposals are so attractive but also so inadequate. In that way, distrust comes to surround claims about the moral possibilities of today's schools.

To be sure, scepticism about moral education is perennial, but this historic scepticism is different from the liberal temptation to isolate schooling from commitment and the conservative temptation to fragment schooling into sectarian ventures. Demanding "relevance," radicals call for revolt, liberals for reform, and conservatives for stability. Potentially the victims of some party or other, school people have yet another reason to erect a shield of moral indifference and to become even more effectively institutionalized. Ultimately, we come to conceive of schooling as literally polytechnical; we focus on skills and competences and pretend to deal only with the factual. Where we cannot avoid moral education, we reduce it to a "subject matter" too or add another exercise in skills development. The myth that skills, competences, and techniques are value-free reinforces this pedagogic illusion. We even come to believe it ourselves.

By contrast, consider the statement of a humanist teacher:

Some who criticize liberal education on the grounds of its elitism press a different argument. They hold that there are "humanist barbarians," that is, persons initiated or learned in the cultural masterworks of the West whose actions contradict the fundamental values implicit in that tradition. In the trauma of twen-

tieth century European history, for example, masters of the classical tradition
are found on both sides of the great divide in moral values. Yet, such difficulties
with moral education are not new. There have never been guarantees of the consequences of any educational system.... After all, Plato suggested that virtue
cannot be taught on the ground that Pericles did not succeed in transmitting
political virtue to his own children. Nevertheless, too much should not be con-
ceded from the evidence that humanistic education does not immunize its students against succumbing to some virulent form of barbarism. The relationship
between educational institutions and their moral consequences is too remote to
permit any firm conclusions. The existence of "humanist barbarians" is a cautionary guard against the illusion that there can be a formal education for morality. It is not necessary to conclude that an education in the skills and substance
of the humanist tradition is not justified by its intellectual and moral results.[9]

Somewhere on the ground marked by the passion of the concentration camp survivor and the humanism of the classical ideal, moral
education can still be found. Happily, the very pluralism and variety
that is so troubling to society is rich and fertile for the middle ground.
Less happily, the abdication of society in the face of its massive needs
defeats schooling all too often, yet our expectations will not disappear. Interesting questions are unavoidable, and moral values influence us whether we will or no. For good or ill, we are shaped by that
second biography when in school.

III

Many of us could agree that moral education may sensibly be ap-
proached from the side of schooling. There, the unfinished nature of
moral education would be neither a surprise nor a defeat. We enjoy
and learn from the unfinished nature of the sciences, the multiple
interpretations of literature and history, the alternative logical and
critical constructions of mathematics. If, therefore, moral education
is naturally part of schooling, we would have located it where a
moratorium can be understood by most of us to be in place—except
when we are advocating polar ideological positions.[10]

On the middle ground, judgements are often deliberately tempo-
rary. We grant students spaces that are not granted us in the rest of our
lives. That is another reason why a factory model is so self-defeating
and why the middle-class drive for achievement is so dubious, and

while we try to connect the second biography with our primary one—perhaps as model, template, workshop, or even mistake, dead end, side road—we nevertheless can let the second biography develop with fewer compulsions about goals and actions. Student life encourages possibilities and experiments. The first-grader draws, paints, molds, sings, and acts, but does not necessarily expect to become an artist; the sophomore plays in a jazz band but does not expect to become a musician; the high-school senior is poetical but does not expect to become a poet. Neither are these spaces found only in the arts, although they yield our clearest images of the second biography. That is why calling them "frills" betrays a deep illiteracy about schooling. Of course, the graduate will enter business, the law, medicine, the retail shop, or the factory. As a student, he or she tries out history or literature, the biology laboratory or the athletic field.

To be sure, this second biography must meet standards of discipline and effort, and it is surely serious or, as the progressives rightly have it, schooling is itself experience and not simply preparation for experience. However, it is differently serious; its decisions and moments of closure are framed and set apart. Conduct and consequences are much more visible, more directly related to intentions, more explicitly subject to criticism and criteria. The second biography is also lived in a world where less is at stake, although as lived it is seriously taken and felt. In it, so much more is opened up to view and so much more of us is exposed. If schooling is a side step, we do not forget that it also calls for a return. Like the released prisoner in Plato's allegory of the cave, we are exposed to the light of the sun but are obliged to return to the darkness.[11] Neither do we forget that the world enters the classroom, and indeed must enter the classroom. When it does, however, it is deliberately transformed, rebuilt for the purposes of learning.

In school, moral education is thus unavoidable and unavoidably experimental. That is why any orthodoxy will come upon moments of outbreak in schools, moments of risk and testing, and suspect schooling. These outbreaks may then be interpreted as the work of the devil or the failures of sinful human nature. Thus unwelcomed and condemned, their educational value is lost. Even traditional and more heterodox institutions cannot, however, avoid the stubborn presence of unfinished moral development. For example, a recent report on Roman Catholic education commented:

Despite their schools' emphasis on traditional moral values, seniors in Roman Catholic high schools may be more likely than their public school peers to engage in shoplifting and drug and alcohol abuse preliminary results from a national study suggest. . . . "The Catholic high school does a good job of promoting important values in kids, particularly in religion. . . . But it isn't as good at preventing adolescent behaviors we want to prevent."

Sister Catherine McNamee, president of the Catholic educators' group, said the study "demonstrates that students don't always follow through on what teachers say."[12]

Schooling, unlike training, does not permit a simple transfer from classroom to practice. In the moral life, that elusive move is very puzzling, although we are already accustomed to its uncertainties in academic disciplines, in student politics, in friendships, and in romance. By locating moral education on the middle ground, we permit, as with all schooling, a richer and more complex appreciation of what goes on just because we have stepped apart from what goes on. When we fail to make the distinction between student life and life, we come upon the seriocomic sorrows of the adolescent and the perspectiveless "realism" of parents. When the student fails to make the distinction, we can at the extremes get the horror of teenage suicide.

We should not be seduced, however, by the attractions of the middle ground. It is not innocent of its own moral point of view. For the middle ground, moral education is a process, and moral values emerge from it as we mature. Metaphorically, we might understand it as the appropriation by biography of the second biography. Extremists on all sides must thus feel the threat of schooling. That is why fundamentalisms of the left and the right desert schooling for training and indoctrination. A commitment to development is entailed in schooling itself, at a minimum the willingness to suspend our "correct answers"—and we all have "correct" answers—for the sake of learning. At the same time, there is always the chance of a troubling scepticism. For example,

A layman or small child with the proper education will also eventually see a proton—without it they will not. But with the proper education they will also see certain moral situations as wrong, and without it they will not. Accordingly, the highly touted convergence of scientific observations versus the divergence of moral observations merely indicates a higher degree of socialization among scientists than one finds in ordinary moral socialization. . . .

Simply put, those who cannot find protons in cloud chambers do not receive Ph.D's [*sic*] in physics; hence their observations are not scientifically relevant. Those who do not see anything wrong with burning cats are, at worst, thought perverse, and their observations survive to count as evidence for the relativity of moral observations. In other societies this order is reversed and religious and moral observations are considered to be more veridical than "factual" ones. That we evidence greater convergence in scientific observations than in moral or religious observations is an interesting fact about how people in modern industrial societies are socialized, but I fail to see its philosophical relevance concerning the reality of moral facts.[13]

Schooling is risky, not least of all because the return to the cave is unappealing and even dangerous. In the cave, blood is shed, moral disagreements persist, and ideological battles are fought. These will not be resolved; we will continue to inhabit a pluriform culture. Indeed, we may expect the multiplicities of things to increase both because our world expands its boundaries and because individuals within it find greater and greater room for movement. That means that moral experience will continue to force conflict upon us. Our inability to put it to rest is also felt and not just observed. Moral pain is not an abstraction. In danger, we will demand unequivocal answers and simplifications as a therapy and as a politics. As these turn out to be misleading, most of us will be driven away from the moral life itself, convinced of its pointlessness.

The cave, in other words, invites a more adequate moral education and at the same time increases the temptations to avoid it. Few of us would quarrel with the need for intelligent moral judgement and sensitive moral values in a world so complicated and demanding. Few of us would deny the need to attend to the moral life itself because of the dangers of amoralism, the reduction of the moral to the conventional, or the displacement of the moral by the technical. However, unexceptional as these general propositions are, only when we feel them as direct demands can we take them seriously. If we do not, a paradoxical blandness, a disturbing indifferentism appears. The first biography cripples the development of the second.

Schooling responds to this modern situation, which is why schooling carries so interesting a burden, but schooling to be effective must remain on the middle ground, and that is difficult to accept. We are all potential invaders. We all try to carry our dearest truths into the world and into the school and to reject the dearest truths of others, yet schools, uniquely in a culture, can be simultaneously inhabited

by polar forces without being destroyed by them. Schooling medi-
ates. Quite literally, it comes between, welcoming advocates without
advocating. In the sciences, history, the arts, it succeeds in putting
together the modern and the traditional, the novel and the inherited,
the popular and the classic. In fact, schooling flourishes in the energies and tensions generated by mediation.

We should not underestimate the difficulties of this view of schooling. It took a long time before schooling began to teach science instead of fairy tales and history instead of propaganda, nor will the
struggles about these ever be over. We still are trapped into mistaking
our own loyalties for the conclusions of critical observation; we still
try to convert our own commitments into objective truths. Thus in
wartime we confuse history with policy, and lose, at least for a time,
the capacity for self-criticism, and, under the threat of the evolving
sciences to our dearest prejudices, we draw ourselves up behind walls
of partisanship. Nonetheless, it is in schools that we can properly ask
what is added to the creation story by the term "creation science"
other than the persuasiveness of the name of "science." At the same
time, we can ask why we have the need to even call it a "science."
Mediation is driven by such questions, by the love of the questioner
for an interesting question.

In the moral life, we want practice, theory, and policy to be tightly
interwoven; and we expect it to happen although we really know
better. Ideological pressures, partisan interests, therefore, are difficult
to evade, and it is difficult to accept the notion that moral education
too is a deliberate interruption where error is not sin. Nevertheless,
we work at intellectually and emotionally acceptable mediating
strategies every day in our schools. Teachers ignore the rhetoric of
certainty, even suspend their own advocacy, in order to meet their
students. Schooling is put at risk when one or another polarity breaks
into the middle ground with uncommon demands, as in the current
controversy over "creationism," or as in the politics of "relevance"
that afflicted the 1960s.

The other face of mediation is a democratic culture where differences are appreciated, and where power is self-limiting. On the middle ground, we need to will the unsettled and suspect the conclusive.
This approach to schooling captures the genius of postenlightenment
societies, that is, pluriformity and individuation. Even those who
hold that moral values are actual and permanent should be able to
accept a classroom process that does not begin with an assertion of

their ultimate and final truthfulness. Since values are said to exist inescapably in the world, honest inquiry must eventually come to them. On the other hand, those who deny ontological status to values can as confidently accept a process that does not begin with a "blank tablet." Experience will force us toward moral innovation no matter what the early learnings from family and church. We notice that schooling welcomes a certain vagueness, but then, no matter what our desires and passions, experience is indeed rough-edged—and nowhere more than in school.

Much as democratic schooling captures our commitment to individual development and our appreciation of diversity, it violates another theme of our age: we are anxious for organization and have a penchant for pigeonholes. From this perspective, the problem of moral education is generated as much by modernists with their bias for measurability as by traditionalists with their passion for final truths. In other words, moral education, like all education, does not fit entirely with the modern temper. As with so much else, we are all of more than one mind. John Dewey put the point in another way when he wrote:

Let us admit the case of the conservative: if we once start thinking, no one can guarantee where we shall come out, except that many objects, ends, and institutions are doomed. Every thinker puts some portion of an apparently stable world in peril and no one can wholly predict what will emerge in its place.[14]

Dewey's comment still applies, and more generally than progressives once supposed. We are all afflicted by the fundamentalist temptation; we all want to make "the case of the conservative." Nonetheless, schooling must fail if its outcome must be assured in advance or if the shape of that outcome must be fitted to our bias for the numbers. That is the risk we accept in teaching the sciences and literature and history. It is the risk of moral education as well.

Notes

1. Several hopeful experiments are underway at Roosevelt High School and Bronx High School of Science in New York City. For some years, similar efforts have been at work at Brookline High School near Boston. Disenfranchised and disenchanted students are being introduced to and are working effectively with concepts of "fairness" and "justice" in what Lawrence Kohlberg and his col-

leagues have identified as "the just community" approach. Too early to evaluate conclusively, the experiments suggest that moral education need not be seen only as another middle-class activity.

2. For a discussion of the "marginal" role of schooling and of its critical purposes, see my essay, "Schooling and the Search for a Usable Politics" in *History, Religion, and Spiritual Democracy*, ed. Maurice Wohlgelernter (New York: Columbia University Press, 1980), pp. 317-40.

3. The notion of putting the school on the middle ground is not only for "radicals" and "reformers." Thus:

To James S. Coleman (1982), "it would appear that the process of making human beings human is breaking down in American society." The same forces that break apart the household as a productive unit, in an economic sense, have broken it as a unit of redistribution of income. The elderly are looked after by external institutions; increasingly the young. Could it be, he asks, that ours will be the first species to forget *how* to raise its young? Coleman resists. (Bronfenbrenner too) resists. In the Ryerson Lecture at the University of Chicago in 1985 he asserts that "the fundamental assumption on which publicly supported education in the United States is based is wrong for the social structure in which we find ourselves today. Perhaps the school should not be an agent of the state or of the larger society, but an agent of families closest to the child." Diversity attracts him: in "the ghetto and the suburb" schooling should strengthen the norms that those parents hold for their children, "norms that parents often find undercut by intrusions from the larger society." He proposes to reverse the "very" philosophy that now governs our schools "public and private."

In Patrick Moynihan, *Family and Tradition* (San Diego: Harcourt Brace Jovanovich, 1985), pp. 192-193.

4. See Emile Durkheim, *Moral Education, a Study in the Theory and Application of the Sociology of Education* (New York: Free Press, 1973).

5. Haim Ginot, quoted in *Moral Education Forum* (Summer 1981): 4.

6. William J. Bennett, "A Cry for Sound Moral Education," *Insight* 2, no. 52 (December 29, 1986–January 5, 1987): 61.

7. Anne C. Lewis, "A Word About Character," *Phi Delta Kappan* 68 (June 1987): 724-25.

8. The attempt to sustain—or better, to restore—a "common culture" is symbolized in two recent texts that are symptomatically highly controversial: *The Closing of the American Mind* by Allan Bloom (New York: Simon and Schuster, 1987) and *Cultural Literacy* by E. D. Hirsch (Boston: Houghton Mifflin, 1987). Recent faculty debates, such as that at Stanford University, about the inclusion of "women's literature" and non-Western materials in the "core curriculum" tell us that the issue is by no means settled, but at least the matter is now debated, and the outcome is not simply assumed.

9. David Sidorsky, "On Liberalism and Liberal Education," in *Sidney Hook, Philosopher of Democracy and Humanism*, ed. Paul Kurtz (Buffalo: Prometheus Press, 1983), p. 106.

10. The notion of a "psycho-social moratorium" was proposed by Erik Erikson in his description of child and adolescent development. Here, I suggest that it made a useful description of schooling. See Erikson, *Childhood and Society*, 2d ed. (New York: W. W. Norton, 1963).

11. Plato, *Republic*, Book 7.

12. Kirsten Goldberg, "Catholic Educators Surprised by Data on Student Values," *Education Week* (April 29, 1987): 1.

13. Richard Werner, "Ethical Realism," *Ethics* 93, no. 4 (July 1983): 669.

14. Joseph Ratner, ed., *Intelligence in the Modern World* (New York: Modern Library, 1939), p. v.

4

Into the Classroom:
Where Shall We Teach?

I

Before we get to the classroom, family and community have shaped our values. However, in the classroom, learning is intentional, and that is the mark of the second biography. The memories recorded in books, films, documents, and pictures enter our experience. Our imaginations populate it with futures, and people are the primary subject matter. When, instead, we focus on this or that "discipline," we fail to educate, and that is as true of history or of mathematics (where it may not be so obvious) as it is true of moral education (where it is more evident). We all know the teacher who tries to "cover" the subject matter, forgetting that the horizon of any interesting study recedes even as we think we have finally reached it. The fact is that we seldom recall what we learned, but instead recall with whom and from whom we learned. Thus, too, the fact that what we do recall is what created and served our interests; we all know the "poor" student who, paradoxically, masters a skill, hobby, or sport.

These are commonplaces of schooling. When we learned, it was a fellow student or a teacher that mediated between alien material and personal development. Connections—initially unknown and often unpredictable—changed instances into events. That is how the past was turned into history and observations into science.

When we mediate between person and idea, we build bridges between strangers that first appear in all their tangle or apartness. When mediation is organized, we call it schooling. If it simply happens un-

intended, and it does, we learn but we are not schooled. The connections, however, are never secured. Events tangle them up again. Thus,
mediation is always a recreation marked by anticipations of moments
when dearly won organization falls apart. That is the fascination and
the anxiety of all learning.

A residual romanticism still worships the self-tutored genius and
the "school of hard knocks." Perhaps "experience is the best teacher,"
but experience is not simply given. It is constructed and reconstructed.
Happenings are not experience, nor is mere data informative. We
organize what goes on with our habits of perception and ways of
naming. We guess at connections before we meet them. We break
into our habits and question our presumptions. When all is said and
done, our abilities to go on knowing are only half-formed until we
find our way into a classroom. There teacher and student, with all
the baggage they bring, come finally to a meeting with each other.

However, if "natural" learning is a romantic illusion, "managed"
learning is a rationalist illusion. No theory, research design, or institutional reform, however incisive, can reach to our learning if the
existential nature of the classroom is unrecognized. Now this should
be obvious enough, yet we make pronouncements about schooling
that ignore the classroom. Rarely are schoolteachers asked to formu-
late proposals for reform. Recommendations for improving schools
seem almost wilfully to ignore them.[1] Even those who criticize this
omission scarcely think to ask students to participate. Academic
research, foundation grants, publications, and plaudits are reserved
for the professorate. Speeches are delivered by the politician. We
may honor "the teacher of the year" or recall a favorite teacher at
class reunions, and we talk about the importance of the student, but
the classroom and those who inhabit it are typically ignored.

If we are going to make sense of education, and certainly of moral
education, we must look at what happens between teacher and student and listen to what they tell us. Now this shouldn't really have to
be said, and yet we go on trying to solve our problems from outside.
We talk endlessly about curricula while the classroom teacher knows
that lesson plans, texts, and subject areas are only a fraction of classroom reality. We offer up this or that organizational model when the
reality is that organization emerges from experience—something we
find out when we change classroom teachers or appoint a new principal. We shouldn't be surprised then that we fail. Teachers, just like
the rest of us, do not like to be told what to do. They rightly suspect

notions that come at them from those who've never met a class or who long ago left the classroom, but the larger part of their resistance comes from the irrelevance of much that is proposed. It doesn't seem to connect with the classroom, and consequently is not convincing.

It is worthwhile then to recapture something of the experience. We entered early in the day, noisily and regularly. We met with stimuli, with distractions, with many things happening at once. We saw our friends. That was the first thing that happened. For some of us—particularly in the adolescent years—that was the most important thing that happened. We reviewed in our minds and perhaps in our conversations our homework, finished or unfinished. Much of that review had to do with our survival that day, less to do with the assignment, and even less with its value. Around us was a familiar set of paraphernalia. Our acceptance of their normality was a tribute to our adaptability. Chalk boards surrounded us; chairs and desks, 20 or more usually facing in one direction, filled the room. Everywhere there were posters and notices, and perhaps an assignment written on the board. Bells rang to signal the changes; a loudspeaker interrupted with announcements or summons. The clock was ever-present. Our time was segmented into "periods" for this or that, periods that, unlike our experience of time passing quickly or slowly, were always of equal duration. The break from period to period was a signal that we were leaving one reality for another—history for English, academics for art, study for recess. We scarcely noticed, having entered into this special reality, how different our sense of time and space was becoming, how different from the other places where we did other things.

The media of classroom exchange were words and symbols—oral and written. Unspoken signals were exchanged too: a frown, a smile, the tap of a ruler on the ever-present desk. At one level, we appeared attentive, whether to a teacher, a film, or a report from a fellow student. At another level, there were whispers, signals between students which, when too apparent, called for a remark, a look, or something more ominous. We shifted in our chairs—more noise. A theme was introduced by the teacher under some familiar rubric like language, history, or arithmetic. From time to time, we paused for recreation. Often, the pause was accidental—a student acting up, a visitor, even a dropped book—and, because unexpected, was welcomed all the more. Periodically we were tested, at times with ponderous seriousness, as in end-of-year examinations. A transfer occurred—with greater or less success—from teacher or book to student. However, the transfer was, only occasionally, a transformation. Then we held onto it, used it, worked with it. More frequently, it was only momentary, and then only as a signal that we had passed by. Typically, student and even teacher, beleaguered by too much to do in too little time, preferred the lesser effort of transfer, simple repetitions that could be measured, recorded, and forgotten. So we were relieved by "short answer" tests and "multiple choice" quizzes. We could play the odds and survive without knowing very much. The teachers, already overburdened, could grade us with minimal effort.

What appeared and what we recall is only a small fraction of what went on. The public agenda of the classroom was often set aside if other realities intruded to make planned activity impossible. Often, even if not explicitly set aside, the lesson announced and the lesson learned were separated as theme and counterpoint; often the lesson announced was simply blocked by other matters.

Perhaps the way to think of the classroom is as an environment where interference is used constructively. A good teacher is a genius at improvization, an "opportunistic planner."[2] A poor teacher is only distracted. In defense, he or she retreats to the announced lesson as if to overpower distraction by insistence on subject matter.[3] When unpacked from the rhetoric of advocacy and rejection, it is this classroom reality that the progressive educator was pointing to when calling attention to "experience" and when criticizing formalism in the classroom.

In the effective classroom, making connections was a multilayered thing. Distraction was converted into lesson; personal agenda was transformed into common discourse and outside "baggage" was brought inside. Learning went on in this kaleidescope process; a successful classroom, more or less, helped to organize what was happening to us. Before the classroom there were fragments. An even more successful classroom helped us to organize our organizing, taught us not only how things might fit together but how *to* fit things together. In a classroom, time was available for trying out different ways of organizing, so, if we were lucky, we learned different histories, alternative interpretations of poems. We learned to tell stories and to make up stories, to see through our own eyes and the eyes of others, perhaps even to feel what others were feeling.

This sense of the classroom is sloppy and disturbing. We prefer to think it has a beginning, a middle, and an end. When we evaluate teachers, we judge them not on what happens and on how they see it, we use, instead, abstract descriptions—"criteria and references"—that package learning and outcomes neatly. The formal lesson plan that many teachers must submit to supervisors is often an exercise in fiction, and sometimes an insurance policy against fatigue and personal distraction. The teacher, in effect, works through the reality of the classroom, and in another world, so to speak, tries to satisfy the unreality of the structure. Apart from the waste of it all, this has its consequences in bad faith, inviting and even encouraging dishonesty.

In our public talk, we identify schooling with curricula and curricula with blueprint. Now this would not be troublesome—there are important uses of curricula and blueprints—were we not also given to reducing the reality of schooling to these skeletons and scaffolds. They do help us organize a classroom and give us markers for a process, so they have a limited but important utility. At the same time, they tempt us to forget that the classroom is first and last a place of meetings.

II

In a classroom we play our roles. A teacher intervenes and a student responds. There is a curriculum—there are really many curricula—that organizes experience. However, organization only points us in a direction. Then we depart from it. We seize upon the intrusions—what we bring into the classroom and what happens in the classroom. We convert intrusion into subject matter.

In a classroom, we try to use everything that happens, everything we chance upon. Of course, we don't succeed, yet a good teacher helps students to be wary of too easily dismissing anything as irrelevant. There are interesting and usable surprises waiting for attention. Even where an intrusion is finally only a distraction, it is an occasion for reforming purposes and recapturing intentions. I have in mind, in particular, teachers in the early grades, in a neglected paradigm of good teaching. They save everything—a bit of scrap paper, a clipping, loose threads, an old hat, empty spools—not knowing when it may come in handy but knowing that sooner or later it will. They go "on vacation" but their attention is always on the possibilities of what they see for the classroom back home. Their counterimage is the graduate school instructor single-mindedly wedded to the "discipline" and so missing out on the classroom. That is why teaching is often best done, strangely enough, among the least mature students.

This image of the classroom is particularly appropriate to moral education, which has as its permanent content the relationships we build and break. The moral quality of relationships: the values associated with them, with how they are constructed and construed, with how we are with each other, and with how we behave toward each other, are the content of ethical inquiry. The language of morals is a language of relationships. We use words like "justice," "love," "cooperation," and other words like "unfairness," "hate," "violation." Even terms like "integrity," which seem to speak to the self alone, would have a different significance were we living on a desert island. We might regret self-deception and deal with mental hygiene, but there would be little urgency to issues of moral judgement and moral conduct.

Many of the interruptions—at times, they almost seem like eruptions—emerge from our relationships in the classroom. Teachers and students compete for authority. Friendship intrudes on duty. Loyalty conflicts with competition. Fairness and equality are problems of participation. The classroom then is rich with possibilities for studying itself, which is why it can be understood finally as its own subject matter. These interruptions obviously break into academic subject matters, which therefore move back and forth between "discipline" and experience. These same interruptions are in fact the permanent stuff of moral education, but in a classroom we do not leave them alone. Happenings need to be converted into moral experience by the active intervention of a teacher, so it is possible to say that morals are "caught" from what the teacher is, and it is equally possible to say that morals are "taught" by what the teacher does.

Moral education, like all education, is the transformation of interruption into intelligence. We try out new connections and relearn how to make old ones. Of course, we can only pay attention to a small piece of what happens. Fortunately, most of our relationships do not need intervention most of the time. We cooperate, follow the rules, do our assignments, meet our goals. When there is a conflict, we simply reassert the rules or the assignment, and most of the time we can proceed until the next interruption, but even this reassertion teaches by calling attention, by labelling, and by giving importance to. Moral habits are thus refined and supported.

At times, however, the interruption is too serious, will not go away, or cannot be suppressed. Then we must stop and attend; we need to "teach a lesson." In the better classroom, interruption is welcomed because it provides a doorway into a student's interests, a student's biography. Making a connection has a chance of being taken seriously and not being dismissed merely as school stuff. With the serious interruption, school matter can be connected to life matter, becomes life matter itself, and can "matter." In the exciting classroom—and most classrooms are exciting at one time or another—the interruption may even be induced. We may play "devil's advocate," act out a drama, introduce a striking anecdote, or offer a disturbing notion. A good teacher intentionally invites interruption.

III

Our image of the classroom, its unpredictability and lack of clear-cut boundaries, may be disturbing, but it is accurate. That is why teaching is so exciting and so exhausting. Only after establishing these existential realities of the classroom can we turn to its rationality. Our habit of thinking—and of teacher education—is the reverse. We build structures, design curricula, and announce goals. Then we "apply" these. However, this logic not only misleads us, but actually invites us to fail. Thus research results and classroom practice seldom connect. Graduates of teacher-training programs find out on their first day that much of what they learned is simply irrelevant. Policy-makers are misled by administrative abstractions, but nothing changes. Reformers, turning to less elusive industrial models, call for productivity and measurability, but that doesn't work either. Paradoxically, we only call for more and more intrusive management. We might be tempted by the recurrent failure of this logic to surrender rationality itself. Instead, we need to base rationality in the classroom.

We do need logic, analysis, argument, and comparison in our pedagogies. There are, to be sure, those who would simply let things happen. Rousseauean romantics, reminders of a sentimental progressivism, advise us only to remove obstacles so that the "natural" goodness of the growing child can emerge unblocked. An echo of this may be heard in the notion of the teacher as "facilitator." There are, too, behaviorists who urge us to manage better by seeking more effective rewards and punishments. For them the organism is a shapeless mass of raw material to be molded by whatever stimuli we can get to work. Behavior modification is a typical procedure. Of course, both give reasons for what they do, but do not see much of a role for reason in the classroom itself. Their views make the classroom passive and nonmoral. They transfer the discussion of moral education into psychology laboratory experiments or policy debate. For the romantic, the moral work was already done by nature. For the behaviorist, morality is an empty category.

We all despair of reason at times. Its uses are embedded in feelings, and we are never entirely aware of why we do what we do. Thus the bearers of reason can be irrational in their rationality, defend territories, exaggerate claims, exclude alternatives. In addition, moral education evokes anxiety by introducing uncertainty and risk where we do not want it. This anxiety grows as schooling undercuts our search for control in a world that seems so perversely unmanageable. While this or that moment of disorientation will pass, the anxiety that accompanies schooling remains.

Reason, at its best, only partially addresses classroom needs: interpretation, comparison, and relations of cause, consequence, and consistency appear amid feelings, hunches, intuitions, loves, and hates. Nonetheless, serious ideas about moral education have in common the uses of reason in the classroom and acknowledge its limitations. Teaching and learning assume that students and teachers can come to know, to think, to be "rational animals."

Reason does not work in a vacuum. It chews on felt problems and works on puzzles, which is why reason can find its way into practice. That makes the world always one more occasion for the renewal of reason. We are a troubled society, but that is not news. We are preached at repeatedly about our failures as parents and teachers, and there is some truth to it. Thus, critics like Mario Cuomo, the governor of New York, pose a problem:

But it's clear today that we need more. It's clear we need to turn to our public schools. They have proven in the past to be one of the best ways we have for exposing youth to the ideals and traditions that form our common heritage.

Actually, asking whether schools should teach values may be the wrong question. The truth probably is that they do it, inevitably, whether formally or informally, deliberately or inadvertently. Silence teaches. It teaches that the choice between good and evil is not important.

Given that, it seems to me that schools should work to make young people aware that some standards of virtue and decency do exist.[4]

Unlike those who despair of schooling or who want to reduce it to indoctrination, such calls to end the "silence" look in the direction of reason, but teachers are not really silent. Why then does it seem reasonable to think that they are? It is in large part because so much of our talk about schooling misses the classroom and because so much of our preaching deals with false expectations. The fact is that moral values are deeply embedded in the daily reality of the classroom. We study history and everything has a history; we learn literature and everything has a literature. We cannot help but ask questions of value. To be sure, we may or may not say we study ethics—and that is worth a political speech or two—but everything we study has its ethics. Neutrality is, in other words, an illusion.

Properly, to do the work of the classroom is to do moral education. That is the wisdom of conservativism. It is why many teachers cannot understand accusations of amorality on the one side or proposals for teaching moral values explicitly on the other. The realities of the classroom and of the subject matter entail a complex structure of moral values. To be sure, these values often only reflect what is out there—or, more likely, what *was* out there. Thus, the call for learning traditional values based in a study of classical and historic literatures relies on the moral nature of schooling itself.[5] The conservative's criticism, therefore, has to do with the failure of the school to speak to its own reality.

In reaction against the mythology of the neutral school, traditional views of moral education are gaining renewed vitality. For example:

In January 1982, a small school district in southwestern Virginia took a step that school board members hoped would correct some of the problems they perceived in their reading instruction program. . . . They turned to Mr. McGuffey's series . . . because, board members said, they wanted some challenging material and because they sought textbooks that would help children to become honest, patriotic, kind, punctual and persistent.

McGuffey's Readers, which teach reading through a series of "improving" stories and poems drawn mostly from other authors, place heavy emphasis on these themes.

"We felt that the children needed more values like patriotism and honesty, that the basal readers were watered down too much. . . ."

Today, although one can hardly argue that a "back to McGuffey" movement is underway, there is evidence of a resurgence of interest in the series that in many ways helped shape the values of middle-class America. For 80 years, *McGuffey's Readers* were the textbooks from which 80% of all Americans were educated (1836–c.1920). . . .

Mr. Baird (Van Nostrand and Company) and others point out also that *McGuffey's Readers* tackle fearlessly the moral instruction that modern texts shun as too controversial. "They have meat to them," said Ms. Murray (reading supervisor, Britol, Va. public schools). "Everything has a moral to it. They say, 'Do something worthwhile today.'"[6]

A commitment to tradition is not, in fact, found among fundamentalists and know-nothings whose attacks on schooling are motivated by a suspicion of schooling itself. They have as little use for history as they do for the life of reason, nor can "character education"—which is not at all identical with character training—be interpreted only as nostalgia for days gone by. If there seems something quaint in a return to *McGuffey*, the classroom teacher nevertheless can respond to the idea of readers that have "meat" to them, and as Dianne Ravitch among others has noted, traditional texts and the "great books" had literary merit and intellectual content, striking in their absence from much that we put before students today.[7] Neither is the interest in tradition limited to recalling the nineteenth century. As Daniel Callahan writes:

A number of recent books provide an occasion to consider that question. . . . In *Tradition*, Edward Shils sets himself the task of trying to "see the common ground and elements of tradition" and to analyze "what difference tradition makes in human life." In *After Virtue*, Alasdair MacIntyre argues that "the Aristotelian tradition can be restated in a way that restores intelligibility and rationality to our moral and social attitudes and commitments." For William Sullivan, in *Reconstructing Public Philosophy*, "Our best hope . . . may lie in reassessing and recovering our civic republican heritage." For Michael Novak, in *The Spirit of Democratic Capitalism*, we need to recall the forgotten moral roots and ideals of capitalism, which lie not in "rugged individualism" but in the "communitarian individual."[8]

Unfortunately, traditional approaches to moral education run the danger of confusing verbal skill with moral comprehension. As we know, very young children can learn rather quickly to recite the "lesson" of a text or draw the "moral" of a story. They are fascinated by new words and can therefore sound like adults and please adults. Of course, they learn to obey "moral" rules, but the moral character of those rules is an adult notion. For the child, a rule is a rule is a rule. Hence, to reduce ethics to rules is to miss the opportunity for ethical discussion on one side and to mislead children about the nature of ethical activity on the other. Their experience is limited, and consequently generalized moral ideas give them too little to work with. We cannot expect children to make abstract judgements the way adults do, something traditionalists may forget because the aura of the eternal clings to ethics, but this does not mean that children are amoral or that they are merely moral puppets. There is moral challenge enough in their world to call for moral activity and to lead to moral development. They can think morally and do morality.[9] It takes time and the activity of teachers and other adults, however, to get them from within the moral world of childhood and adolescence to the less-contained moral world of the adult. Development, in other words, does not simply happen. If it did, the pressure on all sides for moral education which presumes the absence of moral values would be senseless.

The other issue of traditional education is ideological. Whose tradition shall we choose as the tradition to be taught and which traditional values are the traditional values to be taught? Surely, after decades of "consciousness raising," we've learned that the traditions of Blacks, Hispanics, native Americans, women, Catholics, Jews, Muslims, free thinkers—the list can be indefinitely prolonged—do not speak to a common tradition, and many of us have felt the pressure to teach "the Bible" from parents utterly unaware of how many "bibles" there are and how contradictory even the ethical notions within a single bible are. Thus it is that somewhere a selection has to be made. Unfortunately, conservative presuppositions blind us to that fact or else exclude the process of selection itself from the legitimate work of the classroom.

The criteria of selection remain mysterious to teachers and to students. To be sure, scholars can and do offer reasons and justifications, but these are not dealt with as legitimate subjects for the classroom. There is, thus, an authoritarian assumption latent in traditionalist views. The classroom is a directed environment, the teacher an agent for that direction, and the student an object of that direction. The aim of schooling, learning how to judge and to justify judgements, is violated, ironically, by those who are committed to a moral ideal.

Closely related to the call for traditional values is a renewed interest in civic education.[10] If religious and ethnic values are too diverse to be legitimate subjects in a common school, then surely the political and social values of a democratic society are not. A reconstructed "civics" course is brought back to school now that the cynicism of the 1960s and Watergate seems to have run its course. "Irangate" does not appear to have caused significant damage. Patriotism is again a moral possibility. Preference for a U.S. form of government is again intellectually and morally respectable.[11]

Now this is unexceptionable. Surely the essence of schooling is the democratic impulse no matter how compromised in its execution. However, civic education easily turns into rote learning and chauvinism. Thus the occasion of the 200th anniversary of the U.S. Constitution stirred a lively debate. Led, among others, by Supreme Court Justice Thurgood Marshall, interesting moral questions have been raised from the point of view of women and Blacks and other minorities. Viewing the Constitution as a U.S. icon simply will not do.

Civic education may also revert to the tedium of abstract descriptions of government that never was. Aware of this past practice, one report noting shifts in interpretation of the role and nature of the Constitution, said:

The recent efforts to bolster civics instruction are part of a broader national effort, most of it driven by governors and state legislators, to improve teaching in all basic subjects. . . .

"During the 60's we got away from pride in America, and there was a period of debunking American history," said Jack Zuckerman, principal of Public School 6 . . . in Manhattan. "But I think we're coming back. We point out that the original Constitution was deficient in many respects such as denying civil rights for minorities and women. We also point out that, as a basic document to set the stage for our present democracy, it's a wonderful document."[12]

Even a critical civic education would only be a partial response to the need for moral education. Moreover, as with traditional approaches proper, it runs the danger of lapsing into indoctrination. Like tradition, civics education touches deeply into our moral memories, the unspoken curriculum that we learned as infants and children. Since experience inevitably induces moral anxiety, regression to childhood and to childhood's securities is a permanent temptation.

Clearly, neither tradition nor civics is childish, but our sense of them is caught up in loyalties and feelings associated with our earliest experience. Hence it is a struggle to achieve critical awareness and to combine commitment with a necessary distance.

Somewhere in the middle between the conservative and the liberal is "values clarification." We are likely to encounter it in schools that announce that they "teach values," although the popularity of the program seems to be waning. Thinking to leave values intact, values clarification undertakes to help students expose and understand the values they hold. That would seem neutral, even benign. As Merrill Harmin, who along with Louis Raths and Sidney Simon developed the values clarification program, wrote:

The story opens in the 1950s when I began studying with Louis Raths. He explained how some young people, and some of us not-so-young people, suffer from conflicting pressures and models. . . . Raths urged us to assist young people troubled by such confusion. . . . [A] n effective way to do this . . . was to ask students, artfully and acceptingly, questions that stimulated them to think more about the alternatives and consequences involved in choices they faced; that sharpened their awareness of what . . . each of them most prized and cherished. . . ; or that got them to reflect on how they might best integrate their choices and prizings into their everyday behavior patterns.

This sort of questioning became known as the values clarification process.[13]

Values clarification is not immune to controversy. Because of its willingness to expose values but not to express a preference between them, it permits alternatives that in some communities are unacceptable or, worse, immoral. More significantly, it admits, in theory at least, that all moral alternatives have a right to exist. Thus, from a traditionalist and conservative perspective, "values clarification" is not really neutral. It can easily be accused of promoting moral relativism.

Ironically, a similar criticism appears in liberal views of values clarification. These tend to focus on the failure to make the values that it does in fact teach explicit enough to be subject to criticism. Clearly values clarification invokes a number of liberal shibboleths, for example, respect for individual differences, pluralism in social and personal values, and toleration. It would seem that there are no limits, no boundaries that define acceptable versus unacceptable points of view. The only limit is procedural. We can announce our own values; we cannot judge the values of others, and we must be prepared to listen to, but not to silence, each other.

Values clarification is radically individualistic. In contrast to civic and traditional education, which are social and communitarian, it centers on the individual alone. This conveys the message that ethics is finally an activity between one's self and one's conscience. Thus, for example:

What's "values clarification"[?]. . . . [T]he use of questions as an instruction technique in elementary through secondary grades . . . on issues not considered [ordinarily] publicly arguable. . . . [A]s Raths, Harmin, and Simon wrote in . . . *Values and Teaching: Working with Values in the Classroom*, "In a world that is changing as rapidly as ours, each child must develop habits of examining his purposes, aspirations, attitudes, feelings, etc. if he is to find the most intelligent relationship between his life and the surrounding world, and if he is to make a contribution to the creation of a better world." For most of us, this kind of statement would seem almost a truism. But, as Raths et al. pointed out, the very act of such self examination in a classroom may seem menacing to some. . . . "In some communities it may be matters pertaining to religious issues; in some other communities it may be matters relating to political issues; sex is frequently an issue."[14]

Furthermore, confirming this individualist bias, Harmin wrote recently:

I have been working on a somewhat new approach to helping people clarify their lives. Rather than "values clarification" it might better be called "self clarification." It is not based on an outsider asking questions, but rather on procedures we can do each day for ourselves. I see this not as a replacement but as a supplement to the original Raths plan.[15]

Values clarification presupposes a democratic environment but that is, in part at least, the problem these days. Moreover, while moral relativism may serve as a classroom technique or as a prescription for social peace, it is not a carefully constructed moral philosophy. Even relativism must achieve closure on moral decisions at some time, even if only on the procedural agreement that grants legitimacy to all alternatives, but on what grounds can that be justified, since it would seem that all moral views are equally acceptable including the one that would silence all views but one? There is a contradiction then at the root of values clarification which becomes clear when we realize the import of making toleration the moral priority.

To be sure, values clarification is a classroom method, and does not claim to be an ethical philosophy. It has then the strength of utility and the weakness of inadequate theory. It assumes, finally, that methods are neutral. That, however, needs to be argued, not just asserted. The failure to face this issue will, sooner or later, make for a flawed pedagogy.

An unapologetic approach to rationality in schooling has been developed by Matthew Lippman as "Philosophy for Children."[16] A way of developing critical thinking, Philosophy for Children has ambitions as moral education too:

Ethical thinking is impossible unless it is understood as philosophical thinking applied to moral problems and situations. Ethics is not a self contained discipline. Its application requires that the entire body of philosophical techniques be brought to bear on the issue at hand. It requires above all respect for the process of inquiry and analysis.[17]

Critical of those who would teach decision making as an abstract skill, and of those who, like Piaget and Kohlberg, limit children's cognitions to psychologically appropriate "stages," Matthew Lippman approaches the classroom through classical philosophy. Aristotelian premises guide a program that is built around naturalistic functions like curiosity, naturalistic metaphysics like the intelligibility of the world, and naturalistic epistemology like the availability of the world to reasonable inquiry. Philosophy for Children relies on the ability of the child to think logically and to be both disciplined and imaginative.

As with values clarification, Philosophy for Children is classroom-based. It is also theory-rich, but it seems at times blinded by its rationalist presuppositions. Obviously, children reason but reasoning is not a monolithic activity. We can surely argue that we think differently when doing physics versus doing history, or when doing wood-shop versus doing poetry.[18]

In its anxiety to defend the abilities of children, Philosophy for Children also misses the nuances of cognitive and emotional development. It is simply not the case that philosophic reflection is available in the same way to the 3rd grader and the 12th grader. They do their thinking in characteristic ways and with a different content. The younger child does tend to greater concreteness and paradoxically to greater fantasy; the older child does have an ability to deal with abstractions and at the same time with a certain realism. We need not opt for a rigid passage through "stages" to grasp these facts of a teacher's experience, nor do we derogate the child or the adolescent when we admit that they are not adults. Finally, in its desire to have an appropriate literature, Philosophy for Children ignores the richness of existing literatures, one more warrant for the proper and passionate criticism by the traditionalist of our textbook mentality. Philosophy for Children also exhibits, in the extreme, a polemic quality. It is as if only by slaying the enemy can the legitimacy of one's own claim to truth be established.

Clearly every approach to moral education arises within its own history and from the biographies of its proponents. Lawrence Kohlberg's work on moral development theory is perhaps most explicit about its roots. Kohlberg traced his developmentalism to the ideas of Dewey and Piaget, and took his ethics from Kant via Rawls.[19] In a typical statement, he wrote:

Education, said Dewey, is to aid development through these moral levels, not by indoctrination but by supplying the conditions for movement from stage to stage. Dewey's conception of education as movement through moral levels makes it clear that the individual is not born at the autonomous or self-directing level. Romantics like Friedenberg or A. S. Neill see children as born individual, creative, empathetic, and as crushed or limited by school and society. Autonomy, however, is not born, it develops; the autonomous level comes after the conventional. Autonomy will not develop through an education of "do your own thing" but through educational stimulation which leads first to the level of understanding the standards of the group and then to autonomy, to constructing standards held through reflection and self-judgement.[20]

Kohlberg started from a psychologist's research model. Using as his instrument in a pioneering longitudinal study the moral "dilemma" to test for moral development, he identified six moral "stages." We move from stage to stage, from obeying others to autonomy, then from narrow self-interest to universalism, and finally from family and social conventions to principled moral thinking. Because a "dilemma" has no single correct answer, it is said to test for patterns of thinking rather than for substantive moral judgements, and each stage is marked by characteristic forms of judgement. For example, at "stage 3," one of two "conventional stages," we live up to what people close to us expect of us or, more generally, we live up to the expectations of our social "roles" as sons or daughters, as students, as friends, and so on. Moreover, movement from stage to stage is necessarily hierarchical, since no stage can be skipped and since earlier stages must precede later ones.[21]

Kohlberg recognized, however, that moral development cannot be grasped by empirical methods alone. Normative considerations were unavoidable. "Moral development," after all, implies both change and progress, and the latter requires some standard of judgement. For example, autonomy happens later rather than earlier in our lives, but that fact alone does not necessarily make it better or worse. Only when we assign a moral value to autonomy can we identify the move toward it as progressive or developmental, but where does that value arise? This explains Kohlberg's reference to Kantian notions, and in particular to the idea of "justice as fairness" worked out by John Rawls.

A research program on moral development that used dilemmas and identified stages of growth begged for classroom use.[22] Initially this took the form of "dilemma" discussion based on the notion that deliberate intervention should facilitate the move from stage to stage. Elaborate testing and scoring systems that "measured" the development of cognitive moral abilities seemed to verify the fact. Gradually, as questions about the conversion of cognition to action became more pressing, application of moral development ideas to social environments appeared. The most explicit of these was the "just community":

The term "just community" reflects both what is familiar and what is new about the approach. The familiar is Kohlberg's abiding concern for the principle of justice. The emphasis on democratic rule, role taking, and moral discussion are designed both to promote the individual moral development of the participants and to insure the fairness of the educational practice. What is new is the concern for community both as a means for promoting moral development and as an end in itself.[23]

Unfortunately, a puzzle arises when we compare the democratic intentions of the just community with the hierarchical psychology of developmental theory. If the latter is correct, then those further along must think better morally, and hence deserve authority over those who, by nature, must think less adequately. Those furthest along, that is, at stage 6, must know best. This, of course, reminds us of rule by a natural elite, of the "philosopher king" in Plato's

Republic. Consequently, in practice, although less so in theory, there is genuine ambivalence about authority reflected in most of the adults who work with students in just community experiments.[24]

Nevertheless, the just community approach does recognize that, without action, cognition can easily deteriorate into mere verbalism. From within a developmental perspective, others are working out the place of feelings and emotions in moral education. They hold that "justice" is only one moral idea, and that the emphasis on universal law is a result of masculine gender bias in the original research design. They address themselves to other morally laden capacities like caring, loving, committing, and believing.[25] Again, polemic blinds intelligence. It is not really necessary to choose justice over love or love over justice, or to radically isolate the two.

IV

From right to left, moral education in the classroom relies on the uses of "reasoning," and that is the clue to moving beyond these positions. While differing in their psychological and philosophic premises and often claiming to be mutually exclusive, the alternatives presume that the development of cognitive powers, autonomy, and judgement lead to more adequate and effective moral powers. Thus, together, they differ markedly from the presuppositions revealed by the "well-behaved student," yet we do not really know how moral education leads to a more adequate substantive morality and how it, in turn, leads to morally approvable conduct. It seems only an article of faith that these are reasonably connected. Intuitively we see relationships between moral intelligence and moral action, but the work needed to translate that intuition into dependable theory has not yet been done.

The connection between reasoning and morality—a classical problem—cannot simply be assumed, and yet it is on all sides. Part of the difficulty arises from the differing meanings we give to moral knowledge. Thus, some associate moral habit with reasonable conduct and, like Hegel, believe that all knowledge is after the fact. Others, in good Aristotelian fashion, presume a necessary connection between knowing and doing, and so use an expanded notion of adequate knowledge, that is, we cannot really be said to know at all unless we exhibit our knowledge in experience. Nevertheless, moral development, critical thinking, Philosophy for Children, civic education, character education, and values clarification, for all their partiality occupy a common universe of discourse. They are informed by a connection between modern psychology and classical philosophy, and committed to the place of reason in practice.

The differences that appear in debate more often than not reflect the fact that attention has gone to limited areas of moral education in a wider and more comprehensive domain. Thus, Kohlberg's developmentalism echoes classical philosophy; civic virtue can become radical social criticism; values clarification is a doorway to democratic values; and so forth. Different histories give rise to different alternatives. For example, those whose roots are in the classroom tend to be less punctilious about the niceties of theory, and yet find themselves forced toward theory. The psychology laboratory leads toward measurement, but the criteria grow blurred in the hurly-burly of the classroom. Philosophic ethics finds its ideas disturbed because neither motivations nor actions fit neatly into a priori categories. In short, moral education in practice breaks out of the library, the laboratory, and the classroom, and when it does, it becomes both untidy and more interesting.

It would seem sensible then to treat the available alternatives not as warring parties but as openings to a not-yet-established subject matter. Unfortunately, we are more likely to indulge in partisan arguments reminiscent of other ideological conflicts because, however we clothe our advocacies in the language of academia, we fail to catch the ideological regressions that are at play. Thus, for example, traditionalism begins with the belief in objective permanent moral values; the notion of moral dilemma begins with the belief that contradictory moral directives must arise because the word of the growing organism is not fully morally reasonable. At the same time, the traditionalist in the classroom is no stranger to growth and development; the developmentalist is forced to posit some objective value or other. A necessary step in transcending the available alternatives would be the exposure of these varied commitments, the identification of their sources, and the assessment of their adequacy.

Moral education cannot, finally, be resigned to mere eclecticism or a matter of taste. Admittedly it is a vague discipline, and its likely metaphor is the neighborhood. We may predict that this will be a permanent condition, yet we need criteria for inclusion or exclusion from that neighborhood. That takes us to the next step—a look at curriculum broadly conceived.

Notes

1. For example, see National Commission on Excellence in Education, *A Nation at Risk*, (Washington, D.C., 1983); Carnegie Forum on Education and the Economy, *A Nation Prepared: Teachers for the 21st Century*, (New York, 1986); or National Governors' Association, *Time for Results: The Governors' 1991 Report on Education*, (Washington, D.C., 1986).

2. David C. Berliner, "In Pursuit of the Expert Pedagogue," *Educational Research* 15, no. 7 (August–September 1986): 5–13.

3. Research and experience combined, particularly about the effects of changing classroom size, tell us that the teacher-centered classroom is typical, although we know that effective education benefits from participation, student interaction, and peer leadership. In other words, what we know—and what most teachers know intuitively even before being exposed to research findings—is not translated into practice.

4. Mario Cuomo, "Give Hope To Youth: Teach Values in Our Schools," *Newsday*, March 6, 1987.

5. Diane Ravitch, "Where Have all the Classics Gone? You Won't Find Them in Primers," *New York Times Book Review*, May 17, 1987.

6. Susan Walton, "Returning to W. H. McGuffey's Frontier Virtues," *Education Week* (February 2, 1983): 1.

7. Ravitch, "Where Have all the Classics Gone?"

8. "Tradition and the Moral Life," *The Hastings Center Report*, Hastings-on-Hudson, N.Y., December 1982, p. 23.

9. "Stage theory" is a sophisticated and research-tested description of readiness and cognitive/moral development owing its modern form to the work of John Dewey, Jean Piaget, Eric Erikson, and Lawrence Kohlberg. However, the notion that we pass through "stages" is by no means modern. Shakespeare, for example, wrote of the "seven ages of man," and, as we shall see, the idea of "readiness" needs to be corrected to avoid the notion that it is an amoral psychological phenomenon.

10. See, for example, Aspen Systems Corporation, *Educating for Citizenship*, Rockville, Md.

11. See by way of example Kevin Ryan, "The New Moral Education," *Phi Delta Kappan* 69 (November 1986): 228–33.

12. Edward B. Fiske, "With Old Values and New Titles, Civics Courses Make a Comeback," *New York Times*, June 7, 1987.

13. Merrill Harmin, "Values Clarification II," *Ethics in Education*, Toronto, Canada, 4, no. 2 (November 1984): 2.

14. Eli M. Obler, "The Controversy Surrounding Values Education," *School Library Journal* 27, no. 2 (October 1980): 115. See also Louis Raths, Merrill Harmin, and Sidney Simon, *Values and Teaching* (Columbus, Ohio: Charles E. Merrill, 1966).

15. Harmin, "Values Clarification II," p. 2.

16. Matthew Lippman is director of the Institute for the Advancement of Philosophy for Children in Montclair, New Jersey. For a statement of his views and his program, see M. Lippman, A. Sharp, and F. Oscanyan, *Philosophy in the Classroom*, (Philadelphia: Temple Unviersity Press, 1980).

17. Matthew Lippman, "Philosophy for Children: Learning to Be a Moral Individual," *Ethical Perspectives*, New York, Society for Ethical Culture (1975): 2.

18. For an interesting and challenging discussion of ways of thinking, see Howard Gardner, *Frames of Mind: The Theory of Multiple Intelligences* (New York: Basic Books, 1985); particularly part II.

19. See John Rawls, *A Theory of Justice*, (Cambridge, Mass.: Harvard University Press, 1971); also John Dewey, *Democracy and Education* (New York: Free Press, 1966) especially chapters 4 and 5, and Jean Piaget, *The Moral Judgement of the Child* (New York: Free Press, 1965).

20. Lawrence Kohlberg, "Moral Education for a Society in Moral Transition," *Educational Leadership* 33, no. 1 (October 1975): 47. See also his *Essays on Moral Development*, volume 1, *The Philosophy of Moral Development* (San Francisco: Harper and Row, 1981).

21. This description is necessarily abbreviated. For an excellent discussion of moral stages of development see J. Reimer, D. P. Paolitto, and R. H. Hersh, *Promoting Moral Growth* (New York: Longman, 1983), especially chapters 3 and 4.

22. Ralph Mosher, ed., *Moral Education: A First Generation of Research and Development* (New York: Praeger, 1980).

23. Joseph Reimer, "Moral Education: The Just Community Approach," *Phi Delta Kappan* 60 (March 1981): 485–87. See also Lawrence Kohlberg, "The Just Community Approach to Moral Education in Theory and Practice," in *Moral Education: Theory and Practice*, ed. M. W. Berkowitz and F. Oser (Hillsdale, New Jersey: Erlbaum, 1985).

24. A full discussion of this point was presented by Mark Weinstein in an unpublished paper, "Reason and the Child," at the University Seminar on Moral Education, Columbia University, in March 1987.

25. A Harvard colleague of Lawrence Kohlberg's has developed moral education ideas from a feminist point of view and centers her approach on the idea of "caring" and the context of relationships. See Carol Gilligan, *In a Different Voice* (Cambridge, Mass.: Harvard University Press, 1982). From a philosopher's rather than psychologist's perspective, Nell Noddings takes a similar view in *Caring, a Feminine Approach to Ethics and Moral Education* (Berkeley, Calif.: University of California Press, 1984).

5

"The Map Is Not the Territory": The Four Curricula

I

We're never satisfied. We debate "basics," argue about teaching foreign languages in elementary schools, or complain that social studies has replaced history. School boards get in trouble for what they include and for what they don't include. Sex education, internationalism, or the reading of certain books become matters of passionate partisanship. We say that we are too narrowly academic, and then add more course requirements. We urge interdisciplinary study—often without any clear idea of what that means—while demanding that we strengthen the disciplines. We complain that we are doing too little or too much in the arts, or the sciences, or mathematics. What we teach is either too intellectual or not intellectual enough, too practical or not practical enough.

Medieval scholars, no doubt, argued the merits of the "trivium" and the "quadrivium"; the nineteenth-century university struggled to shift from "natural philosophy" to modern science; the progressive school fought for the inclusion of shop, home economics, drama, music, and art along with the "3 Rs." Given the passionate quality of these debates, we might conclude that we could really find out about schooling in catalogues, course descriptions, text books, and lesson plans—which is a little bit like judging a restaurant by its menu and a cook by his or her recipe book.

To be sure, catalogues help us when we're looking for vocational training or a course on Shakespeare, and textbooks sum up the routines of a subject matter. What we say about what we teach—what we ordinarily call curriculum—is a clue to our intentions, but it only gives us an outline. In fact, most of what we teach and learn does not find its way into our talk at all.

Important as a certain realism is for all schooling, it is particularly important in moral education. We watch a child meet geography, science, or mathematics for the first time. We catch the moment when he or she learns to read. We sense the excitement and feel the mood of discovery. Moral education suffers by contrast. Moral values are already a part of us when we enter the classroom at age five or six. Cooperating, being fair, obeying rules, and telling the truth are all quite familiar, so moral education is "boring" and must begin with destabilizing the familiar. Fortunately, although doing so is painful the changing realities that mark the move from infancy to childhood and from home to school insure insecurity and doubt. At the same time, our temptation is to protect, to keep safe. Thus our inclinations work against moral education, yet without acknowledging the urgency of challenge in moral education as readily as we do in science or social studies, the classroom can only be a muddle of competing moral certainties. We may moralize, but we do not teach.

We convey moral lessons without always knowing that we're doing so. Therefore, we need to work at making them visible. Patterns of conduct, structure, and authority are curricular as much as the language we use to talk about them. Curriculum includes what we do not say and what we do not call attention to. Our silence is also a lesson. Even when we believe we are only approaching the schools as taxpayers or as potential employers, we are practicing curriculum. We popularize professions like law or degrees in Business Administration, or downgrade other professions like teaching, social work, or nursing. Schools are sources of national pride or national shame, as when we respond to Sputnik or put our own man on the moon, but politics and economics turn in on the school too, and are very much a part of the course of study.

Curriculum has many faces. Ordinarily, we think of it as what we find in classroom schedules, in subject matters to be "covered"; in degree programs, in "majors" and "minors," and in professional requirements, but curriculum is also found in the things we do for other than teaching purposes. The former is at least exposed to criticism. The latter, since it is often not understood as curriculum at all, does not come in for scrutiny. We see it as a matter of politics, economics, psychology, or organization. We argue the merits of using schools to allocate labor, to promote racial integration, or to meet international competition, but we do not pay attention to these as curriculum. Nonetheless, our students know who is and who is not in the classroom, and catch the messages of "tracking." Students, listening in on the debate as it were, make judgements about career or social policy; at the same time, they learn about moral values.

We know that literature or history forces attention to moral choices. Students and teachers cannot read Hamlet or Lear, Eugene O'Neil or Arthur Miller without exposing conflicts of conscience. They cannot encounter the Declaration of Independence or Tom Paine's *Common Sense* without raising issues of loyalty and liberty. Choices are everywhere: in the classroom, on the ball field, in casting for a school play, in student government. In fact, there is no way to avoid leading the classroom into unforeseen moral territory.

What we usually call curriculum unfolds into a variety of curricula, and that depends in no small measure on where, when, and to whom it happens. "Position" and social neighborhood for student and teacher—that is, role and status—shape the announced course of study in unannounced ways. A values clarification "lesson" on sharing, co-operation, or truth telling will be strikingly different when taught in a middle-class suburb or an urban slum. Talk about "competition" will be one thing if the class is made up of seniors anxious about college admissions and another for freshmen eager for a new environment. Our moral rhetoric these days will sound the same—we all watch the same TV shows and pick up common cues, for example—but the references and the meanings will be different. The texts may be identical too, but our reading of them will not be. What we study will be reported differently by student, teacher, administrator, consultant, parent, and policymaker. What is evident to some of us may be mysterious to others. This tells us that the distinction between an announced and an implicit curriculum is often situational and positional.

A curriculum may be "thick" or "thin," depending upon how complicated the background experiences the students bring to the classroom. Teaching strategies will vary with readiness, so the announced curriculum returns at different biographical moments. For example, we deal with the facts and values of sexuality in elementary, junior high, and senior high grades and, in a sense, we really do sex educations.

However, curriculum is not haphazard, although there are accidents enough in schooling. Therefore we try to capture our intentions by a more and more adequate description of it. That gives us a language for talking with each other about what goes on, and helps us judge the effectiveness of what we're up to.

The announced curriculum itself may be "implicit" or "explicit." For example, every school claims that it teaches good citizenship and fair play. At the same time, it embeds this teaching in activities without providing for reflection. That leaves the moral process implicit even though intentional, for example, as portrayed in intramural sports, citizenship awards, and patriotic celebrations. The lessons of the announced curriculum may also be masked by other priorities like job placement or college admissions. The classroom situation then cannot simply be analyzed into announced and unannounced, explicit and implicit courses of study. Neither the implicit nor the explicit curriculum is a single thing.

In trying to understand what we are teaching, we also have to account for our own and our students' beliefs and assumptions. Complicating the situation is the presence of common values and differing, even conflicting, particularist values. For example, conservatives and liberals share the common ground of a democratic society, but depart radically from each other ideologically and metaphysically. At the same time, the interplay of the common and the particular reshapes them both. Conservatives give both recognizable and idiosyncratic meanings to democratic values; liberals do the same thing, so even the common ground is ragged, and even the particular grounds are connected.[1] Furthermore, this pattern of accommodation and difference is itself part of the implicit curriculum. The conservative counts on the sociality of the liberal and vice versa.

Whether the curriculum is implicit or explicit depends too on our roles as students, parents, teachers, and administrators, and thus on the positions from which we perceive the classroom. A shift in role, say from teacher to administrator or from student to student leader, may well make explicit what was once implicit. A shift in social values or public agenda may well hide what was once out in the open. For example, feminism makes a husband's role as a "good provider" morally dubious, so we may not talk that way any more in a "woman's studies" or "gender roles" course, but may well continue to play the part—perhaps now a bit uneasily. Curriculum talk thus looks critically at the problems of rhetoric and reality. The interplay of the implicit and the explicit shows up too in our shifting moral horizons. Class, caste, geography, and community set up or tear down our hopes for career or for advanced study.

Educational philosophies and the metaphors at work in and on curriculum lead to greater or lesser degrees of "self-consciousness" too. By directing our perceptions and energies, they even lead us to value differently the explicitness and the implicitness of curricula themselves. A traditionalist, for example, may well rely on an intuitive curriculum for moral education. Thus Aristotle maintained that the good man is virtuous "by nature." The children of the Enlightenment, by contrast, call for a self-consciously designed course of study.[2] A teacher's style or a school's climate will tend to stress nuance or planning, spontaneity or deliberateness.

When we look at curricula in this plural way, we avoid the illusion that moral education can ever be entirely planned or entirely felt; entirely taught or entirely caught. The reality and the fascination of schooling arises from the fact that teaching intends but learning departs. Thus, for example, what looks like eclecticism—the use by teachers of many different approaches—may well be an appreciation of classroom realities and not a token of anti-intellectualism. Finally, attention to the complexities and pluralities of curriculum helps us avoid reductive conclusions, for example, that schools are "nothing but" agents used by authority, class, or what have you to control future generations; and even as we rightly complain of the overburdened school, we should not forget that the course of study everywhere has initiated the young, marked rites of passage, had vocational intentions, and conveyed the loyalties of the tribe.

II

A curriculum is spoken in many languages, and all languages are at a remove from experience. They are *about* what is but *are* not what is, so discussion of curriculum is language about language, and thus doubly distant from the classroom. At the same time, we need to find our way around, hold on to things after they have vanished or changed, and share with others. Consequently, language is necessary. We keep Wittgenstein's warning in mind. "The map is not the territory," and analysis is not experience. Then we are in a position to talk about moral education and its four curricula. We are reminded, too, that experience is continuous, a flow that is interrupted, perhaps, by moments of self-consciousness. As with any analysis, that which is analyzed has its own unities, its organic connections.

A

A first curriculum is not peculiar to schooling, and yet it is how we are schooled for all future schooling. We might think of it as ideology, but that carries too much of the political and the polemic fully to capture our hunches about it.[3] We might conceive it as "myth," but a first curriculum is not only an explanatory "story" that is taken as true. Similarly, we might point to the way "metaphor" is taken to be "real," as in "economic man," the "individualist," or the "age of faith," yet ideology, myth, and metaphor are much too self-conscious for a first curriculum.

We are able to name the metaphor, myth, or ideology, and that speaks to a first curriculum for other people. In fact, these are terms outsiders use. Our own first curriculum is, as it were, transparent to us. When we examine it in other places and times, we readily see its myths, metaphors, and ideologies, and can understand it as a course of study. We realize, too, that parents, priests, politicians, and pedagogues convey a first curriculum by what they are even more than by what they do or say. Unlike implicit curricula which can move into or out of consciousness, a first curriculum remains hidden. We can infer that it is present in us from its presence elsewhere. We cannot know how it is present in us. We human beings are not all that different from each other. We live within very similar patterns of culture and society, and we are, though not completely, shaped by our biology.[4] Thus we are warranted in thinking that what we find in others will likely be found in us, but whatever our guesses and conclusions, a first curriculum in us is still an inference.

"Hidden" as it is, a first curriculum cannot be held up to consciousness, since our very consciousness is formed by it. Even when we see it at work in others, it is through the lens of our own consciousness. Thus, it is prior to—and hence, genuinely "first." It is a first curriculum that shapes our perceptions and establishes the syntax and grammar of our overt and covert languages.[5] A first curriculum is shared. We learn from it, through it, that we belong to an identifiable group. We are equipped with its symbols and with interpretations of the symbols of others. We quite literally come to be as members, come to have a particular consciousness, for example, in the way that Eskimos "see" and name 100 shades of white.

A first curriculum carries its legitimacy along with its reality. Its messages are unchallengeable since the very way in which messages come to us is shaped by our membership, so when questions that touch upon it are raised—by a nonmember, an alien presence—we are noisy but inarticulate. We feel a deep disquiet and are moved to suppress the questions and the questioner, yet we do not understand the vehemence of our response, particularly those of us whose commitment to "rationality" makes all questioning legitimate. We are not able to figure out why we are so uncomfortable. If, as rarely happens, a successful challenge is mounted, then we experience a break in the world, a departure into unknown territory along with a violation of what is felt and held as sacred. Hence, we can also infer the presence of a first curriculum by the defenses we muster, the anxiety, anger, and aggression we exhibit. Since, on the other hand, teaching is always a form of criticism, a teacher is forced to be both member and stranger. Suspicion of teachers is thus rooted very deep in every culture, although some may handle it by turning teacher into shaman. Schooling is thus an inherently risky business.

In a first curriculum, moral values are marks of membership, telling us who is and who is not a participant. Values are not initially instruments for making judgements and decisions. A rationalist bias that sees values as functions and goals is, in other words, itself the message of a first curriculum, but when we are able to call it a "bias," we also have a clue that a first curriculum is in transition. That is why we can make what was once hidden visible; nor are we simply making the remarkable discovery that emotional qualities must attach to morality—rationalists know that too. The point is that even the shape of our moral ideas and feelings is a message of a first curriculum. As vehicles of identity and group solidarity, moral values carry with them an untouchable quality. This, in no small measure, accounts for the weight we attach to them, the guilt that accompanies violation, and the shock we feel when encountering the sociopath who is not so much immoral as nonmoral. It is why we are so incorrigibly antagonistic when meeting other moralities. It is the reason, perhaps, why an analytic study of ethics seems to have so little connection with actual conduct, so liberals are very like conservatives in their moral uses if not in their moral rhetoric, and radicals are notoriously reactionary in their moral puritanism. It is no accident, either, that comparative moral study is usually rather thin.

A first curriculum shapes teachers, students, and the institutions in which they work. Thus moral education encounters a hidden reality. It is not surprising then that curricular reform circles back to familiar outcomes and that the battles we fight for this or that change are often about minute differences. Indeed, what we are prepared to call schooling is itself the reflection of a first curriculum. For example, compare traditional apprenticeships, tribal indoctrination, polytechnic institutions, and liberal arts schools. We assume the rightness of some essential meaning for "schooling," and measure all others by it. Inherited forms are reconstructed to a normative model. When, for example, some parents propose to teach their children at home, we reject it as unthinkable, deride it as regressive, and finally force it to become like all other schooling. Even the parents acquiesce, saying they will simply do the job better. To be sure, we give good reasons for all of this, but what counts as good reasons is in part a function of a first curriculum. Even without good reasons, we would still do what we felt we had to do and feel justified in doing it, so language is replete with phrases like, "That's the way things are," or "I don't know why but it feels right."

It is the presence of a first curriculum that justifies us when we say that values are "caught, not taught." However, a first curriculum is never perfectly transparent. We feel its presence in our resistance when we meet the convincingly inexplicable. It seems to become visible. This, however, is not a sign of enlightenment but of some "new" first curriculum that is working its way into our reality while remaining successfully hidden. A first curriculum reveals its presence at moments of conflict or transition, in the presence of invention and innovation, in the interaction of class and caste, or when cultures meet. Thus we speak of "culture shock," "deracination," or perhaps "anomie." Our age is one in which we rub shoulders with variety and change, so we are at one of those historic moments when a first curriculum seems tantalizingly visible. However, even as more and more is exposed, what is hidden is still well hidden. Since exposure for its own sake is a modern temptation, a first curriculum gets to be even more deeply buried and more strongly defended. Paradoxically, then, our age is one of expanding awareness and expanding irrationality at one and the same time.

Few of us live entirely within a single culture or society, but if the idea of a first curriculum makes sense, we all have some kind of primary membership. The unavailability of boundaries thus induces an unbearable tension. Finally, then, part of the difficulty of moral education in our time is that we are, as it were, possessors of and possessed by a plurality. Since consistency is not a necessary feature of that plurality, we often hold on to contradictory realities simultaneously. We are sceptics in science and dogmatizers in religion, lovers at home and aggressors in the marketplace. Compartments must come naturally to us.

Each of us is both a participant and an observer, an actor and an object. We are, in a sense unique to human history, multiple persons. At the same time, cultures more and more seem to look like each other; but if our guesses about a first curriculum are accurate, then that similarity of appearance can be only superficial. If a "global village" should ever come to be, only then will a first curriculum again become comfortably transparent.

I confess to a feeling of vertigo as I reflect on this first curriculum. I experience its effect as an "infinity of mirrors," yet self-reflection is a feature of human experience too, so even in the isolations of tribal life, a first curriculum did not entirely capture us. A look back at legends and stories of exile and expulsion signifies the permanence of marginality in human experience. We are, in others words, unfinished beings. A first curriculum is, however, the basis on which the rest of moral education is built, and from which it seeks, never successfully, to depart. Thus, moral education both preserves and destroys; it is comfortable yet frightening, both a giving and a taking away. A first curriculum reveals the dialectical character of all moral education just because it is hidden. When we come across pedagogies that are neat and logical, we know by that fact alone that they have missed the point, and we soon find out that they do not work in the classroom.

A first curriculum is unavoidably first, psychologically and developmentally. It follows that moral education is, of necessity, mysterious at its roots, and that moral understanding is a struggle that must be waged but that cannot be won. In a troubling way, then, moral education must be partly unintelligible.[6] There have been times when this suggestion would not have been troubling. The moral life was simply to be revealed to us. Moral values might be discovered by reading signs and omens. We, however, are not contented to let a first curriculum remain invisible even if we know that it will. The way we are shaped forces us to strive after self-consciousness and nourishes the illusion of visibility. Our enlightenment roots push us toward this illusion, yet we have to admit an impenetrable quality at the heart of our enterprise.

Inquiry, discovery, criticism, and analysis are partial, and remain so. In turn, this leads us to recognize, far more than reason-based strategies suggest, that "experiential" and "intuitive" learnings underlie moral education. Unfortunately, these terms have become frayed around the edges, yet the awareness that a first curriculum is at work tells us that any effort to capture moral education through language and logic alone cannot succeed. Moral education is first existential: what and who I am precedes what I do, think, and know.

B

A first curriculum is hidden: a second curriculum is implicit, but it is not necessarily hidden. It moves out of the shadows into visibility and back again. Thus, a second curriculum may be hidden from students but known to teachers. We might be tempted, therefore, to conclude that values are "caught" by students and "taught" by faculty. Hence, we locate the place of the teacher as a moral model. Unfortunately, our experience is never quite that neat. For example, the informality of recent faculty costume suggests instead that teachers have "caught" what students have "taught."

A move from role to role is accompanied by a move toward visibility or invisibility. Policy-makers, administrators, teachers, staff, and students play parts that carry intended and unintended moral values. An institution both happens and is designed. Thus, schools corroborate or subvert truth telling and obedience to legitimate authority, loyalty to peers, and competitive success. These are both announced and implicit, celebrated in rituals like "award assemblies" and preached in commencement addresses. We do not, however, always catch on to the fact that the unintended import of our structures may contradict our announcements and our ritual practices. A second curriculum accrues over time. These layers of practice deposited in institutional history are not likely, therefore, to be coherent at all. We recognize the possibility by advising: "Do as I say, not as I do."

The rules and the way we enforce them, for example, those that are said to guide professional relationships or those that set limits for students, are also curricular. However, we are often blind to this, and debate the rules' effectiveness but not their pedagogy. Not having grasped the nature of a second curriculum, we reveal our inability to control moral education. For example, the invitation to participation increases the number and types of participants in governance. A small administrative committee is easily managed; a large student–faculty assembly is unpredictable. Therefore we value participation and at the same time shift "real" decisions to invisible groups. Both the small committee and participatory democracy then teach unexpected and undesired lessons. Student and teacher, finding inconsistency between democratic pretention and demagogic conduct, learn to manipulate school reality and to develop survival techniques. They also learn what counts as moral and immoral.

Under conditions of grossly unequal power such as exist in classrooms, two types of interpersonal maneuvering almost inevitably arise. The first involves seeking special favor . . . moving close to the sources of power during off-hours and behaving in ways that cause authorities to respond favorably. . . . In adult society this strategy leads to the practice of bringing the boss home for dinner. The classroom equivalent . . . is the traditional apple for the teacher.

A second tactic . . . involves the practice of hiding words and deeds that might displease the authorities. . . . The secrecy that frequently develops . . . is aligned . . . with the authority sturcture. . . . Teachers keep secrets from their principals as do students from their teachers.[7]

In short, institutional arrangements in schools and elsewhere are elements in a second curriculum. Architecture, financial practices, appointment policies—none of these is merely functional.

A second curriculum is never only explicit for adults and only implicit for students. Policymakers, for example, may be closed off from the way the school is for its students and teachers. They easily confuse the rhetoric with the reality of authority, so they find themselves to be ineffective and don't know why. Schools thus become mysterious, even threatening to them. They are put in a position of helpless power and so strike out blindly. Certainly, an insider/outsider distinction operates to keep parents and politicians at arms' length. Policy-makers thus learn lessons of scepticism; parents become suspicious; teachers become fearful. When added to memories of childhood experience, the classroom recalled in all its ambiguity, it is not

surprising that this scepticism, suspicion, and fear are accented by resentment. Thus, the contradictory images of teachers in our culture—
both as keepers of our "most precious possessions" and mock figures
of impracticality, absent-mindedness, and even irrelevance. When the
moral lessons of a second curriculum are even more dissonant, resentment turns into active hostility, yet because so much of it is taught
and learned implicitly, we are hard-pressed to explain where it all
came from or to do much about it.

Student life has a second curriculum too, one that is explicit for
students and "hidden" from teachers. We glimpse it when we observe
how new students are initiated into the values of the tribe by earlier
generations. Typically, high-school teachers remark the passage of
freshmen who were once childlike and accessible. Subcultures within
a school—"jocks," "grinds," and the like—are particularly visible with
their special languages, symbols, and ways of walking and dressing.
Adults find these alternately silly and threatening. Above all, adults
are excluded not so much from the behavior as from the meanings.
Thus a teacher who tries to be "one of the boys" is often regarded as
foolish. Finally, a student's second curriculum teaches teachers, administrators, and parents to keep hands off.

Similar considerations apply between teachers and administrators.
The promotion of a faculty member is greeted with congratulations
and envy. Quickly, however, a second curriculum takes hold. Exclusion and inclusion appear. The former teacher complains of alienation
from his or her colleagues. The latter are puzzled by the appearance
of sudden differences of conduct not simply traceable to new respon-
sibilities. During labor negotiations, for example, a second curriculum teaches anger that is usually out of proportion to the actual
events.

A second curriculum is never unified. Its complexity together with
its unintended outcomes makes it problematic for moral education.
We never play only a single role or live only in a single structure. A
teacher is also a parent, friend, counselor, and confidant; an administrator may teach, and so forth. To the impenetrable quality of moral
education imposed by a first curriculum, we add the consequences of
a second curriculum that follow from our multiple roles and their
implicit messages.

Unlike a first curriculum, however, a second curriculum is not
transparent, so it is possible to address it deliberately. For example,
opportunities occur when political bias becomes visible, when a con-

tradiction between claim and practice explodes into destructive conduct, or when cultural conflict exposes the passing of a first curriculum. The call for "participatory democracy" on campus in the 1960s
was one such moment, and the struggles for racial and gender equality
were others.

In other words, a second curriculum can be made explicit, so it is
not surprising that we should try to manage the second curriculum.
Typically we pay attention to structural reform, to governance, to
the cues of relationship we find in the languages we use to address
each other, and to ritual celebrations. For example, under the in-
spiration of recent management theory, we pay attention to non-
operational features of corporate life, to a corporate "culture" that
appears in schools as well as in businesses.[8]

Effective principals are symbolic leaders who pay attention to small, but important, cultural details. Consider a few: reflecting desired values in everyday
speech and behavior; anointing heroes and heroines among teachers, students,
and parents who exemplify these values . . . setting aside time in faculty meetings to talk about values and philosophy; taking the time to introduce a new
teacher, student, or parent to the school's culture. . . . Little things like these
can, over time, transform a school's culture. And a strong culture will yield
dividends in learning achievement, morale, personal growth, and other indicators
of school performance.[9]

To be sure, efforts to manage a second curriculum are by no means
only recent or only corporate. Traditional expectations that teachers
would serve as moral exemplars were codified in conduct and dress
codes reflecting a managerial intention. The implicit values of rational
management underly the efforts of moral development theorists and
practitioners to move students and faculty toward democratic governance in "just" communities and "fairness committees."

However, a second curriculum takes many shapes, and is always
implicit to someone even in the most completely self-conscious strategies for going public. For example, the late Lawrence Kohlberg and
his colleagues took "justice as fairness" to be self-evident. Discussion
of the idea with students in demonstration projects was typically
political, semantic, or psychological. Seldom, however, was the
premise itself put to question. Role presuppositions continued too.
Teachers were still teachers, and thus carried authority with them in
virtue of roles that were not internal to a just community; students
did not escape being students. The connection between justice and

equality was not explored. At a less sophisticated level, students of corporate culture—for example, in management seminars—talk within the presuppositions of that culture: organization, profit, competition, privacy, and so on, and advocates of moral exemplification seldom raise the question of moral ambiguity, the fact that we always exemplify more than just one consistent set of moral values. A second curriculum then is intelligible, available to criticism, and still elusive.

C

Ordinarily, when we talk about curriculum we are only referring to a third curriculum. This is the domain of the "3 Rs," of history and social studies, science and mathematics, and art and physical education. Teacher training is specialized to pieces of territory, and assignments vary with the specialization. As we say, we teach reading, physics, or literature; we "cover" a subject. Even where we say we're teaching students—and this is unfortunately only a cliche except perhaps in the early grades—our priority is the content and the mastery of some "body of knowledge." At first glance, then, a third curriculum is explicit, visible, manageable, and familiar. We breath a sigh of relief.

It's not that easy, however. The announced stuff of history, geography, literature, or science keeps growing. The teacher struggles not only to keep up but to account for the depth and richness that he or she experiences in the teaching and reteaching itself. It is not surprising then that a teacher will tell you that he or she is always running just to stay in place, and it is not surprising, either, that moral values should play a secondary role in the third curriculum.

Unfortunately, disciplines are elusive for other reasons too. They don't come with neat boundaries around them, although text books give the impression that they do. To be sure, a discipline has its own integrity or it would not persist, yet even the technical languages that carve out intelligible domains turn dumb at the edges of inquiry, and we are forced toward invention and metaphor. For example, I think of the mathematical and linguistic adventure that is particle physics these days, or of a cosmology that seems quite comfortable with "black holes" and "quarks." Innovation and evolution, and not only in the sciences, are driven by insights, "paradigm shifts," that force reperception of fields of inquiry.[10] Even so-called "normal science" these days is forced across the boundary lines, which accounts for the frequency of hyphenated disciplines. The situation with humanistic studies is no less blurred, although our familiarity with ordinary language and history tends to blind us to how much they spill into each other. For example, a notion like "structuralism"—that formal fixed patterns persist across cultures, time, and genres—is broadly applied in anthropology, linguistic analysis, literary criticism, and history.[11] In use, a discipline borrows from other disciplines, although not always explicitly or critically. It acquires new meanings and complexities. Because of this blurring effect of experience, we frequently talk of "interdisciplinary" schooling; because of the habits of the discipline, the talk is seldom effective.[12] Furthermore, because of limits on time and energy, neither the fruit of inquiry nor the fascinations of blurred edges easily find their way into the classroom. A third curriculum, in other words, is not as available as it seems to be at first glance.

A third curriculum does, however, make its contribution to moral education. History or literature often stir up interesting questions. Issues of loyalty or duty come along with studies of the Pilgrims or the Middle Ages, or tales of King Arthur. Questions about democratic values are embedded in U.S. history. Perhaps less obviously, aesthetic values are conveyed by mathematics as we catch a sense of appropriateness or fittingness, and these are not unconnected to themes that appear in discussions of equity and justice. The sciences, and not only in their applications, present us with moral choices. Moreover, moral values have a way of appearing in many disciplines at once, so the concept of justice shows up in Greek tragedy, in the U.S. Constitution, in welfare economics, and in folk music. Inquiry itself carries with it values of truth seeking and truth telling along with less obvious values of sociability and cooperation. A teacher knows that disciplines are morally charged. He or she also knows that, from a moral as well as an epistemological point of view, a discipline is never contained only within itself.

Nonetheless, we cannot conduct moral education only through a third curriculum. In part, this is simply a consequence of having too much to do in too little time. It is also a token of our failure to teach teachers to be moral educators. Specialization exacts a high price—but not only in moral education. For example, it is a struggle to get both teachers and students to accept the notion that correct grammar and spelling is as much a requirement of the history or science class as of the English class.

However, features of a third curriculum itself block our realization of its moral potency. Within a discipline we talk with a special language. We signal a shift between disciplines when we change languages. We become aware of boundary problems when language turns dumb, and so are alerted to the need of further inquiry, of cross-disciplinary activity, and even of inventing new disciplines. We judge whether or not we have been successful by how we meet or fail to meet disciplinary expectations—an effective literary interpretation, a coherent historical explanation, a validated scientific hypothesis. However, neither the language that trains us into a discipline nor the expectations that tell us the training has been effective necessarily incorporate a moral dimension. We can do the work of science, literature, history, or what have you without doing the work of ethics.

Moral values are present by implication in everything we study. At the same time, they are external to what we are studying. The subject captures our interests and our energies; its problems take center stage for us. A primitive example is the typical textbook. In its introduction, there is usually a nod to moral or other values, but it quickly leaves these for the subject proper. Frequently, too, moral values are taken to be self-evident in what we are studying and so, at most, are only named. Finally, moral values may indeed become problematic— for example, as in the move from biology to environmental studies or as in the moral failure of legal education at the time of Watergate— and then they are addressed in an ad hoc way as a problem of the discipline. Once solved or, as likely, muted by time, moral values recede into the background again, and we get back to the real buisness of study. A third curriculum, in other words, turns to explicit moral values only momentarily, only when connections of various kinds are called into question either from inside or outside the subject matter.

Usually a third curriculum tends to leave moral ideas where they were. We may plan for them in connection with this or that lesson. We may introduce historic cases that exemplify moral puzzles relevant to a field of study as in discussing the Emancipation Proclamation or Wilson's "Fourteen Points." Moral values themselves may become issues for a discipline as when a field breaks new ground or in facing questions of academic freedom, but the "solution" is absorbed and returned to an implicit moral substratum of the discipline. Moral criticism is thus a sporadic activity in a third curriculum. We lift it up for attention when necessary, work on it, and then include it as part of the axiomatic structure or, less formally, the habits of the discipline.

For example, we institutionalize "peer review" in reporting experimental data or rules against "conflict of interest" in public-policy research. The moral underpinnings of such disciplinary presuppositions, however, do not come in for much discussion. The priority is still the subject matter.

Ironically, ethics is itself such a subject matter, just another specialty. Thus in graduate study we focus on skills of analysis, the history of the discipline, and questions of technique and academic competence. Moral performance is utterly unconnected to the study of ethics as a discipline. Given the priority of the subject matter in a third curriculum, even a teacher with the best of moral intentions must have other interests. When to these are added the natural puzzlements of a third curriculum, with its blurred edges and confusing territories, it is not surprising that moral education should be a secondary feature of ordinary study. Even in the elementary grades where the boundaries and the specializations are more fluid, attention to language, arithmetic, and social studies tends to mute moral education.

It follows that we cannot rely on a third curriculum for moral education, although that is the hope of those who would simply depend on humanistic study to do the job. Conservative suggestions for teaching moral lessons from within the curriculum cannot help but fail after an initial flurry of interest dies down. It also follows that it would be inappropriate to try to force a third curriculum toward a larger role in moral education. We would meet the resistance of teachers' legitimate commitments, and we would run a serious risk of debasing study itself.

D

A fourth curriculum is explicitly committed to moral education, although it cannot stand alone. It ranges from the traditional to the modern, and from moral literacy to moral analysis. In religiously inspired schooling, it may be taught as moral theology or as religion itself. In secular schooling it wears a variety of costumes. At its simplest, a fourth curriculum appears when we schedule time and attention for the study of moral issues as such. Therefore, since every tale has its "moral," we stop and teach a "lesson." Unaccustomed to the activity, this derivative approach tempts us to moralism. We are quite likely to spend our time delivering a sermon, exhorting to virtue, and resorting to indoctrination. We may open up the neighborhood with values clarification or probe more deeply with dilemma discussions. Even in the most minimal departures from a third curriculum, however, we are breaking into the usual course of study. Benefits flow from attentiveness, coherence, and the evolving competence of teachers and students. Dangers arise because moral education can easily become another specialty, another piece of a third curriculum.

A fourth curriculum develops its own agenda. Of course, it includes ideas like justice, rightness, goodness, fairness, and cooperation, and skills like reason giving, objectivity, and principled thinking; but it is shaped by realities to which it must respond and that it cannot predict and plan for. Questions are brought into it by student and teacher. Thus, it is not opportunism but necessity that directs a teacher toward the realities of events and needs. Of course, any teacher will do this on occasion. In a fourth curriculum, however, the occasion is not merely tolerated but actually expected and invited. Similarly, any discipline is responsive to events, but much the larger part of its work is already circumscribed by its own issues. Even where an event directly attaches to a lesson—for example, an election and a U.S. history course—the event is only illustrative of a prior agenda, a way of dramatizing or focussing it. The use of that event is optional, more a matter of teaching style and pedagogical judgement than a construction of the agenda itself.

By contrast, responsiveness builds a fourth curriculum that grows from the world as felt and experienced by the participants as and when they experience it. Thus, an issue of fairness in teacher–student relationships is not merely an example of the problem of justice, which is how one might view it in teaching an ethics course. Instead, that issue of actual relationship goes to construct our very grasp of the problem and our definition of its meaning. Our knowledge of how justice was served elsewhere is a tool for encountering the actuality of our own experience, our own problem. The ordinary practice of a third curriculum is inverted. That makes the planning and coherence of a fourth curriculum always problematic, and the lessons of a fourth curriculum seldom duplicable. Its possibility and usefulness, even more than elsewhere in schooling, therefore, is for the teacher who is able to depart the comforts of predictability.

Together with its own history and its responsiveness to the world as felt, a fourth curriculum draws upon the moral content of the other curricula. For example, student government is not only to be performed but also studied. Similarly, community service—a project much talked of these days—is not only to be practiced but also examined. A fourth curriculum thus intersects with the others.

At the points of intersection, we also find ideas for working on the other curricula. For example, nature study is a typical theme for young children, but it loses its preciousness as moral issues posed by environmentalism appear. I've watched first-grade teachers work with children in a local park or a playground, planting a vegetable or a flower garden against the background of traffic, noise, tall buildings, and noxious smells, but it is striking that now they include these in a study of the systemic impact of human conduct and choices.

We look for other intersections. Since the late 1960s and because of the problematic features of modern democracy, we are particularly sensitive to issues of student self-government. This should help us to enlighten the study of political science and history. Unfortunately, that doesn't happen often enough. In a fourth curriculum, we then call for a moral criticism that helps reconstruct both a third and a second curriculum. In other words, just as the materials of a fourth curriculum emerge from the others, so the concerns of a fourth curriculum reflect back as criteria of choice and judgement.

Finally, a fourth curriculum includes the acquisition of moral literacy and decision-making skills. Thus, it is connected to history, literature, and logic. It has, however, its own skills to teach. Indeed, these provide language and structure, a particular frame of reference, for dealing with what spills out of the disciplines and providing responses to events and relationships. For example, because a fourth curriculum is explicitly moral, contradictions between rhetoric and practice are a persistent theme. Therefore, its skills—moral reasoning, moral analysis, moral history—are instruments of moral diagnosis.

The sources and functions of a fourth curriculum guarantee that it will be a center of controversy if it is effective. It must stir up questions of power, for example, between school and home, or teacher and student. It invites community controversy by dealing with moral issues posed by sexuality and textbook censorship. The sporadic nature of our attention to moral education is partly explained by the discomforts that a fourth curriculum must generate. In a sense, we would prefer to ignore the whole business. When this is impossible— when the contradictions are too great to be ignored—then we pay attention once again but from within a hostile and anxiety-filled situation. Our habit, really, is to get back to evasions as soon as possible, and since the crisis must pass, we succeed. Gradually, however, the gap between rhetoric and practice opens again. Once again we accuse ourselves of moral incompetence. We complain of a loss of values, of moral insensitivities, of moral illiteracy. The cycle moves, and a fourth curriculum reappears. New proposals for moral education are made or old ones are dug up. Of course, being crisis-driven, our ideas about moral education lack the benefits of consistent development. It would seem then that a fourth curriculum would best be a regular feature of schooling, but there is little likelihood that this will happen until our views about it change.

Notes

1. It is not surprising that Marxist theorists have taken the lead in discussing the role of ideology in schooling. The notion of "false consciousness" clearly invites that discussion. However, they are not alone. An excellent article on the subject is Henry A. Giroux, "Theories of Reproduction and Resistance in The New Sociology of Education," *Harvard Educational Review*, 53, no. 3 (August 1983): 257-93.

2. See Werner Jaeger's study of education as character development in *Paideia: The Ideals of Greek Culture*, 3 volumes, translated by Gilbert Highet (New York: Oxford University Press, 1945). The study begins, "Education is the process by which a community preserves and transmits its physical and intellectual character. For the individual passes away, but the type remains" (p. xiii). Compare this view with Rousseau's *Emile* and with Ivan Illich's recommendation that we "de-school society."

3. See Karl Mannheim, *Ideology and Utopia*, vol. 2 (London: Routledge and Kegan Paul, 1936), pp. 2-4.

4. Recent discussions of the relationships of gender and sexuality have revealed what was once hidden and transparent. Until recently, we confused sexual behavior, sexual identity, and gender roles. It turns out, however, that this "natural" connection between genitalia and conduct is neither as natural nor as determined as we presumed. That it was a presumption—a first curriculum, I would suggest—is rather evident now. Similarly, criticism of gender-based language suggests the presence of a first curriculum too. See an excellent discussion of these themes in Alison M. Jaggar, *Feminist Politics and Human Nature* (Totowa, N.J.: Rowman and Allanheld, 1983), especially chapter 2.

5. Clearly, the notion of a "first curriculum" is suggested by many sources. Anthropologists in the study of culture identify "folkways" and "mores." In a critique of how science is conducted, Thomas Kuhn speaks of "normal science"

and "paradigm shifts." See his *Structure of Scientific Revolutions* (Chicago: University of Chicago Press, 1962). Dorothy Emmet in *The Nature of Metaphysical Thinking* (London: MacMillan, 1953) identifies root metaphors as the way through which we grasp reality. A recent article, one of many, addresses "The Deep Structure of Schooling" [Barbara Behnam Tye, *Phi Delta Kappan* 69 (December 1987): 281-84].

It is not important for our purposes to argue for or against a universal linguistic and cultural structure. (See, for example, M. Piatelli-Palmarini, ed., *Learning and Language: The Debate between Jean Piaget and Noam Chomsky* (Cambridge, Mass.: Harvard University Press, 1980), pp. 23-54. What is important is how much learning goes on out of sight and, in a sense, out of mind.

6. To move beyond reason is a disturbing thought, yet we recall that even Plato, idealist and ideologue of reason though he may have been, left the final step in reaching the ideal to an intuitive process; that is, ultimately wisdom escaped rationality. See Plato's "Symposium," *The Dialogues of Plato*, 2 volumes, ed. and trans. B. Jowett (New York: Random House, 1937), pp. 334-35.

7. Philip Jackson, "The Daily Grind. . . ," in *The Hidden Curriculum and Moral Education*, ed. H. Giroux and D. Purpel (Berkeley, Calif.: McCutchan, 1983), pp. 55-56.

8. An excellent example both of the approach to and interest in corporate climate is found in T. S. Peters and R. H. Waterman, Jr., *In Search of Excellence* (New York: Harper and Row, 1982), especially part 2, "Toward New Theory."

9. T. E. Deal and A. A. Kennedy, "Culture and School Performance," *Educational Leadership* 40, no. 5 (February 1983): 14-15.

10. See Kuhn, *The Structure of Scientific Revolutions*, chapters 6 and 7.

11. See Claude Levi-Strauss, *The Savage Mind* (Chicago: University of Chicago Press, 1966); and H. E. Gruber and J. J. Voneche, eds., *The Essential Piaget* (New York: Basic Books, 1977), chapters 39 and 40.

12. Howard B. Radest, "On Interdisciplinary Education," in *The Philosophy of the Curriculum*, ed. S. Hook, P. Kurtz, and M. Todorovich (Buffalo: Prometheus Press, 1975).

6

The Fifth Curriculum:
Thinking about Thinking

I

With the four curricula we do much, but not all, of the job of moral education. The first curriculum establishes the moral ego; the second, citizenship; the third, literacy; and the fourth, comprehension. We learn to be, to act, to know, and to judge. The four curricula also help us build a framework for locating alternative approaches to moral education and explain the apparent eclecticism of first-rate teachers in the classroom. We may still choose sides between developmentalists and traditionalists, cognitivists and emotivists. Despite the temptation to exclusive choices, however, these views are only partial. To be sure, cognitivists, whether liberal or conservative, tend to build from the third and fourth curricula, and emotivists from the first and second, yet except when we are posing for an audience at a professional meeting or a school board hearing, we know that moral education is always an affair of conduct, feeling, and mind. The best proponents of any point of view tend to spill over from curriculum to curriculum. The conservative includes both lessons from literature and history and the experience of moral modeling.[1] The liberal shifts from dilemma discussions to just communities and moral climate.[2] Indeed, it is only those driven by an anxiety for formulae who try rigidly to turn insight into cookbook recipe.

We also need to avoid the temptation to peaceableness, which is very great in a field marked by attack from without and sectarianism within. We do need to exercise judgement but we cannot do so in ad-

vance of living in the classroom itself. The first curriculum, for example, tells us to expect to be inarticulate when facing moral realities
whose existence for us can only be inferred but whose existence for
others can be identified and described. In fact, the better we do our
job, the more likely that we will encounter inexplicable discomforts
and even irrational angers when serious moral comparisons are made
between cultures, castes, and classes. The first curriculum thus guides
our efforts away from arrogance, self-righteousness, and naive ration-
alism. It delivers the message that moral education must attend to
anthropology, mythology, and poetry. The second curriculum calls
attention to the moral environment and brings to awareness the moral
side of what are intended to be nonmoral structures and arrangements. The third suggests the moral possibilities and limits of academic subject matters. The fourth offers choices for direct moral
instruction.

Still moral education will elude us. We again hear echoes of Socratic
ignorance. Of course we expect moral education to be a matter of
unfinished business because generations follow generations and need
to be initiated into the values of the tribe. Moral education is unfinishable business, however, because of the nature of the field itself:
the hidden qualities of the first curriculum, the positional shifts from
implicit to explicit of the second, the attention-driven character of
the third, the perspective limitations and event-responsive features of
the fourth.

Finally, then, an analysis of the four curricula leads us away from
managerial illusions in moral education, but it does not, thereby, lead
us back into copy making or into some version of moral intuitionism.
Instead, we are led to reflection in moral education, to the role of
philosophy, a discipline that sets out to consider in an organized way
all unfinished business.

II

We should not be surprised to find that views of moral education—
or anything else for that matter—fit with the predilictions of their
proponents. Thus psychologists offer psychological ideas, historians
offer historical ideas, and philosophers offer philosophic ideas. In
practice, however, we are all psychologists, historians, and philosophers. Thus, it is no surprise that we all use philosophic considerations

in our work—sometimes openly, more often implicitly. Developmentalists may believe their psychology of stages is independent of values and cultures. Using the notion of "formalism"—that is, patterns of thinking without regard to the content of thought—they claim scientific objectivity and moral neutrality. This so-called formalism, however, blocks consideration of philosophic and ideologic presuppositions by denying their presence, yet developmentalists, like the rest of us, are forced to do something with moral substance too, so they adopt a normative notion like "justice as fairness" or "caring" but scarcely recognize the need to examine it or to do philosophy.[3] Traditionalists are no different. At their best, they provide apologia for, but little criticism of, democratic society and Judaeo-Christian values. Values clarification theorists rely on liberal notions like the "marketplace of ideas"; and so it goes. . . .

Unfortunately, this back-door importation of some arbitrary philosophic point of view makes for uncriticized and even naive assumptions. The clearest example of the danger of trying to do philosophy in passing was Lawrence Kohlberg's use of John Rawls's "justice as fairness" and his rejection of utilitarian notions of ethics.[4] No doubt, Rawls's work is a major contribution to recent ethical thinking, but it is by no means an unchallenged philosophic position.[5] However, some two decades after the debate around Rawls's ideas started, moral development theory still uses "justice as fairness" as if it were the philosophic equivalent of a scientifically established hypothesis. Similarly, defenders of Judaeo-Christian values select from a vast and contradictory literature without exposing their criteria of selection. Typically, they talk of "biblical values," but they do not answer the question, "Which bible and why that one?" Revelation and history may be used as justifications, but these are only other names for faith and custom. We still need to know if we are hearing the word of God or the devil. Liberals forget that John Stuart Mill—and every serious philosophic liberal since—put limits around the utilitarian calculus and the free market of ideas when he posed the rhetorical question: Would you rather be a "pig satisfied or Socrates unsatisfied?" Thus elevating the humane gentleman to moral ideal, we suit our bias but not our reason.

Philosophic thinking is unavoidable; good philosophic thinking is not, but just what do we mean by philosophy? Philosophers themselves are less than helpful. The subject is resigned to the specialist. At the same time, philosophy inevitably plays a role when we are doing moral education in the classroom, and we would subvert the classroom if we expected students and teachers to take their philosophy unchallenged from the expert. To be sure, philosophy is a technical discipline requiring years of preparation and study. Under the influence of its modern Anglo-American practitioners, philosophy has become almost exclusively a sophisticated technology producing elaborate linguistic and logical analyses. To the outsider, this activity often seems to be "much ado about nothing."[6] On the Continent, and increasingly everywhere else these days, philosophy has rediscovered substance, particularly under the influence of existentialism and of real-world issues in medicine, business, religion, and politics. This, we suspect, is why Rawls's creative combination of analysis and substance is so fascinating and important. Gradually the sharp boundary is disappearing between "metaethics"—theories about theory—and "normative ethics"—what we ordinarily think of as ethical questions. Nonetheless, we are still left with a discipline that remains a mystery to most of us.[7]

At the same time we find the renewal of a historic countertheme. Philosophy is also an amateur's game, and it is available to anyone who proposes to think clearly, long, and arduously about serious problems. This Cartesian influence is still alive, the effort in Descartes's *Meditations* to strip away all presuppositions and to work further and further back to personally reach the minimum truths necessary for life and being. To be sure, both views of the "career of philosophy"—to use John Herman Randall's phrase—have been around since Plato. In Plato's *Meno*, Socrates and the slave boy together create the dialogue.

Without derogating the complexities of the discipline—which must emerge from taking thinking seriously—all philosophic thinking has a common genesis. It begins when we learn that nothing is ever only what it seems to be. We want to talk with others about this and about the questions that follow. Furthermore, observing, talking, and questioning are characteristically human activities. Typically, we organize and reorganize our talk into patterns and pictures. In other words, curiosity, rationality and sociability underlie the doing of philosophy. Not least of all, doing philosophy is fun, although the minutiae of argument often defeat its pleasures. Thus, we can do philosophy plain or fancy, as a professional speciality or as a reflection on ordinary behavior, and, indeed, the two are connected and instruct each other. Daily life throws out problems for thought and calls back thinking to experience; technical analysis shapes that thinking and improves our ability to understand and even, on occasion, to solve problems.

There is a double place for philosophy in moral education, too. Our addiction to back-door philosophic presuppositions begs for criticism. Such presuppositions have been imported into theory and practice without sufficient thought, and so we have work to do. That would appear to be self-evident, although psychologists, religionists, politicians, and teachers are quite successful in ignoring it.

However, there is another role for philosophy in moral education. It shows up when we step back and observe what we're doing in the classroom.[8] We realize that the four curricula are caught in our existing assumptions, structures, and metaphors, and this is true whether we are liberal or traditional. The four curricula are, as it were, inherently conservative. Exciting classrooms—and there are many—do not depart from social and cultural realities very easily. For example, dilemma discussions pose issues between property rights and human rights, but do not probe deeply enough to ask whether and how property rights are human rights, or whether and how rights themselves can be justified. The situation is even more obvious with values clarification. Traditionalism clearly presumes the correctness of the culture, so even where comparative study is encouraged, the palm is awarded to our own beliefs. Critical thinking tries to leave matters of substance alone by focussing on informal logics and the development of reasoning skills, yet, by avoiding substance, it in effect sustains the cultural and social values that are around us.

At the same time, when we work only within the four curricula, we come across things that block moral education. For example, feminist critics like Carol Gilligan have challenged the centrality of the notion of justice in moral development theory. In the name of "caring," they have exposed assumptions, forced rethinking, and identified limitations on all sides, including their own. Similarly, traditionalists, when made uncomfortable by fundamentalists who nominally inhabit the same moral neighborhood, are forced to expose their criteria for selecting from within tradition. They come to recognize the inadequacy of their defense of such selection, which helps account for a growing conservative literature on ethics and moral education.[9] Civic education discovers that patriotism, democracy, and individuality are ambivalent terms. The apparent simplicity of teaching Judaeo-

Christian values is blocked by sectarian judgements about what those values are and are not. For liberals, structural reform and social policy—for example, attempts to use student government and community service in moral education—open up a Pandora's box of unforeseen consequences. Participatory democracy and affirmative action, for example, run into demagogery and racism. In other words, we discover that the problems of moral education are not simply a result of living in a pluralistic society. Many of them would exist even if we all belonged to the same church or party.

It is not simply a matter of partisanship. Teaching raises questions that are unanswerable within the four curricula. This leads us from standard practice to philosophic reflection:

There is no such thing as a neutral educational process. Education either functions as an instrument which is used to facilitate the integration of the younger generation into the logic of the present system and bring about conformity to it, or it becomes the "practice of freedom"—the means by which men and women deal critically and creatively with reality and discover how to participate in the transformation of the world.[10]

We need not be revolutionaries to suspect the conservative import of the curricula. The classroom itself has a way of upsetting the comfortable. The first-grader confronts the teacher with "Why?" over and over again. The seventh-grader bursts the bonds once felt so securely as boundaries. The high-school senior, caught between parental expectation and personal desire, renews questions of justification. We may try to restrain them by insisting on our authority, yet the questions persist.

Thus, the four curricula reveal their own inadequacy and lead us into a reflective process. When this process is denied, then curiosity turns to cynicism, tedium replaces pleasure, and schooling becomes a chore. On the other hand, if curiosity is merely indulged, then schooling is trivialized in the name of freedom. Anything goes, and critical intelligence vanishes. Reflection is an intentional and disciplined activity—to think about our own thinking and to think about our own moral judgements, choices, and reasons. We are led thereby to the "fifth curriculum."[11] At the same time, we are resistant and even fearful. Philosophy—the death of Socrates is its symbol—is felt and known to be a threat:

It is dangerous to reflect seriously upon the nature, origin, and consequences of beliefs. The latter are safest when they are taken for granted without reasoned examination. To give reasons, even justifying ones, is to start a train of thought—that is, of questionings.[12]

III

Many of us doubt the possibility of doing philosophy with children and teenagers, so we need to make the fifth curriculum as tangible as we can, particularly too since philosophic thinking is by nature abstract. A simple and puzzling human activity is at work. We step back from what we are up to and look at ourselves while we are doing whatever we're doing. This is precisely what we mean by reflection: the ability to think about ourselves thinking. We stand to one side as critics of our own actions. Thus, we may express surprise, asking, "Was that really me?" and disappointment, claiming, "That wasn't the real me." However, we also take a third step. We ask whether or not our surprise or disappointment was justified: "Is my surprise surprising?" Conscience, for example, is a judgement on our actions, but we also talk about a good conscience, a clear conscience, or conscientiousness. We are able to put together a broader sense of things under the name of character, that is, the person whose conduct and conscience consistently meet some moral standard. We are able to step to one side historically, too. We are able to judge our judgements in rather complicated ways.

Philosophy organizes this reflective process. We learn to ask layered questions like: "What am I doing when I do physics and what must I do in order to qualify as doing physics?" and "What am I doing when I do ethics and what must I do in order to qualify as doing ethics?" Working with such questions, we get criteria that tell us whether in fact we are doing that activity and how. For example, "creation science" doesn't meet the criteria for being a science; it does not offer hypotheses that can turn out to be false. It may still have merit and be truthful, but its truth is not scientifically verifiable truth and its merit has other sources. Reflection keeps the questions coming. Perhaps we try to figure out why we give priority to one source over another; say, to religion over science or science over religion. Similarly, if we mix up morality and legality, we find out that we cannot talk about good and bad laws, that is, we can't apply moral criteria to statutes if what is legal is moral and what is moral is legal. Consequently, we will fail to do ethics, and we will fail to do law.

Now this activity of stepping to one side needs nurture and skill. It is not easy for us to get beyond our initial fascination with appearance and reality, but it is also true that reflection on reflection comes quite naturally to us, and it is this process that informs the fifth curriculum. Paradoxically, we can even overdo the perfecting of skills and block reflection, so it doesn't hurt to remind technical thinking of its mundane origins. Adults thus often have greater difficulty with philosophy than do children because we've acquired habits of thought and language that block reflection by seeming to solve its problems. If we already "know" what's scientific or what's ethical, then we give answers even if we put a question mark after them. For example, we say, "That's so, isn't it?" All we're really asking for is acquiescence. We thus cross the line from schooling to preaching, from educating to indoctrinating.

Absent the fifth curriculum and we are likely to find a dull classroom. We've all seen the impatience of adults—we've all been impatient adults—when answering childrens' questions. We give the "obvious" answers, and still the child comes back at us with the same question. We repeat the answer; the question returns. Finally we answer absolutely and curtly. The child surrenders, having learned that questions aren't worth asking. We've all asked "teacher questions"—questions to which we already know the answer. We want the student to play a guessing game with us, to find out what's in our minds. We're not really asking questions at all but imposing our authority in the costume of inquiry. As Gareth Matthews notes,

There is a certain innocence and naivete about many . . . philosophy questions. This is something that adults . . . have to cultivate when they pick up their first book of philosophy. It is something natural to children.[13]

At the same time, the fifth curriculum is not available without effort. Naivete may be a source of the fifth curriculum, but raw curiosity and intellectual innocence are not substitutes for the work of its development. The fifth curriculum has an agenda just as the other four do, it is the critical examination of what we are learning in the other four.

In the four curricula, we teach moral values implicitly and explicitly. We apply moral ideas and extend them to novel situations. We develop moral priorities. We acquire moral language. We learn the uses of moral reasoning in the face of moral conflict, for example, consistency in applying rules, due process, and fairness. We learn the requirements of moral argument: what counts as a good reason, as evidence, and so on. The skills, the literacy, and the sensitivities developed in the four curricula need, however, to be reflected upon, and indeed, each curriculum (as we have seen) drives toward an edge where it is confused and silent. Moral history, argument, and reasoning are used to work on themselves. Thus, for the fifth curriculum, the subject matter becomes the other four.

We all learn from the first curriculum the lesson that it is and remains hidden from us. At the same time, the fifth curriculum tells us: expose everything to reflection. This opposition can meet constructively in us. The resulting tension forces our imagination into thought experiments. We construct alternative moral worlds. We conjure up stories, parables, utopias; we turn to literature, to history, and to anthropology. We act out moral drama by trying to be rather than simply play the role of the other.

The first curriculum still cannot be other than hidden from us, so we return from our experiments and still are what we are. We cannot escape ourselves, and yet we have self-consciously, willingly, tried to do so by taking standpoints that help us deal with our frustrations and with the unknown sources of our valuations. We thus know ourselves better by knowing what we cannot know. We need not wait only on strangers to challenge our arrogance, to locate our irrationality. We can become, as it were, our own stranger by taking sides, by entertaining the alternatives. The first curriculum still leaves moral autonomy problematic. We learn, however, that we can push to its limits, and we can better understand our own.

We can expose the structures, presuppositions, and limits of the other three curricula. For example, we cannot undertake reasoned argument without decision on some moral givens, but these are givens—axioms, assumptions—and cannot themselves be justified. How, then, shall we understand them? The fifth curriculum also helps us think through the notion of the moral dilemma, the availability of equally cogent but different and sometimes contradictory moral judgements. For example, we ought to be loyal and we ought to be truthful, but we cannot be both in a given instance. We must decide, but the available arguments are not determinative. Among other things, we are thereby led to probe issues of belief and of commitment, to discover the logical commonality of the secular and the sacred. The notion of decision itself comes in for reflection too. The fifth curriculum thus opens up an expanding moral landscape.

Critical reflection also has emotional consequences. We experience the frustrations of being unable to get behind our assumptions. We sense the same struggle in others. Thus, we argue the issue of abortion rights, yet with all good will and imaginative role playing, we reach a point of difference that we cannot bridge. There is an impenetrability to all moral education to which we respond with feelings, reactions, and concerns, so the fifth curriculum provides us with a reflective content for the notion of respect. The process of moving into the place of the other person establishes a moral ground for human relations between those who radically differ from each other. When done with integrity and care, we tangibly share with each other the pain of moral inadequacy.

Without the fifth curriculum, our moral freedom is at risk. As Christian Bay wrote in a related context,

Political education . . . must be sharply distinguished from conventional processes of schooling which emphasize the training and molding of minds and habits of thought, not the liberation of each intellect. Every major school system in the world surely seeks to produce useful citizens with skills and inclinations to carry out pre-ordained social roles; people who quietly take their assigned places within the established order and are not disposed to ask whether it ought to be improved on. The dialectical arts are generally neglected; as most school officials and teachers see it, their task is not to emancipate young people's minds but to harness them as a vital resource for society such as it is.[14]

The fifth curriculum is not the ultimate achievement of moral education for which the other four are only preparatory. The five curricula at their best occur simultaneously as a teacher tries to bring them together. For example, an adequate study of history needs a sense of the history and philosophy of history as well as a knowledge of history's content. The same holds true of other disciplines and of other inquiries. Indeed, the failure of so much of schooling to capture the student is rooted in a truncated view of the course of study.

The opportunities for bringing things together are many, the practice is less frequent. How many of our students are never helped to identify the "individual" in seventeenth- and eighteenth-century thought as a metaphoric bridge between literature, politics, physics, and economics? Similarly, we seldom help our students connect scientific metaphor with structures in poetry, music, sculpture, theater, and painting. What we miss is an instructed intuition that appreciates the tissue of experience in a time and place; nor are curricula only backward-looking or static. Students live through events in the present; they have history, politics, economics—but hardly anyone tells students that this is so. Like Molière's "bourgeois gentleman," they speak prose all their lives but do not discover that they do. Ironically, we reinforce the separation between discipline and experience by calling the study of our own time and place "current events."

The organization of a discipline must appear to students as utterly arbitrary unless its givens are explored. Why, for example, the special place of chronology in history when many interesting alternatives suggest themselves, like organization by theme or type of event?[15] Moral education too has its substance and its presuppositions, its data and its structure, its performance and its reflections. Thus, the five curricula appear as the generalized form of all inquiry, and the fifth is where inquiries come together in an examination of inquiry itself. At that point, reflection forces us to realize the artificiality of so many of our academic boundary lines, the interwoven character of knowing and valuing.

IV

Holding up a mirror to a mirror can be a difficult and frustrating activity. Underneath it is our primitive curiosity. We enjoy questions and puzzles, are fascinated with fantasy, story, and drama. Young or old, we all playact, and so experiment with being the other person and with the experience of otherness. Rooted in the quintessentially human, the fifth curriculum, however, is not just serendipitous rumination. It is committed to the organized development of moral intelligence. An independent human being needs to be morally good, to know why that is the case, to know how to know about such matters, and to know how reliable that knowing is. Anything less is inadequate.

At the same time, learning cannot be forced. Readiness makes sense. Perhaps we force a child to read because we are anxious parents or are responding to anxious parents. To be sure, a young child can learn the letters and even put words and sentences together. Later, however, that child will have trouble attaching reading, comprehension, and pleasure to each other. Forcing the pace will embed emotional resistance, and it will show up. Reading then will become more, and not less, difficult.

However, from a common sense about readiness in individuals we have inferred other ideas that are problematic. Given our bias for the numbers, we transform the notion of readiness into a sequential structure with measurements as tokens of passage from state to state, as in test "norms" for various "grade levels." We then organize curricula by presumed levels of sophistication and thinking processes by age and stage. We perceive knowledges hierarchically, the least complicated to the new student, the most complicated to an elite minority. Finally, we objectify this "division of labor" as epistemological truth and as social organization. These ages, stages, and levels then become independent realities, and their mundane rule-of-thumb sources are forgotten. What begins as a commonsense classroom intuition becomes a problematic wisdom. This structure is not morally neutral, however. It carries a potent judgement about who can and who cannot be morally adequate.

By way of example, let us take a brief look at "moral development" and Philosophy for Children as instances of a debate about development.[16] The debate, unfortunately, is often quite noisy. Advocacy exaggerates the differences. Nevertheless, serious moral issues are at stake. If a child is morally educable only to the limits of whatever stage he or she is in, then he or she is morally culpable only to that same limited extent. One then should as little blame a child for not "respecting the rights of others" as a rock for falling. That being so, it follows that much of our blame and punishment cannot be morally justified, and that obedience to those who do know and who are culpable is legitimate. But if a child cannot assess the knowledge or culpability of those who do know—if he or she could, then obedience wouldn't be a moral necessity—the child becomes the subject of the power and position of others, and this subjection is now morally justifiable. The instruction of those at "lower" stages by those at "higher" stages would seem to be the common sense of the matter, yet, whence the authority of those at "higher" stages—except, perhaps, from those still "higher"; and what is really meant by "higher"? The issue finally comes down to the benevolence or malevolence of the powers that be, and which only they—and not their subjects—are competent to judge. However, since to be a judge in one's own cause is inherently dubious, a position that turns a child—or, in fact, anyone at a "lower" stage—into a moral incompetent is finally morally doubtful. A "pure" stage theory of moral development thus cannot stand without reference to some nonpsychological standard of judgement. We seem to be driven to a Platonic republic, to the rule of the moral elite.

Now it may be true that the child is morally incompetent as just about all adults assume, although the evidence is by no means conclusive. Perhaps the moral status of a child is like a patient's incompetence. This would require a professional and parental ethic to safeguard children's interests, to limit teacher's autonomy, to counteract the natural temptations of authority, and so forth. Simultaneously, it would require lifting the burden of moral judgement, of praise or blame, from the child. Liberals and traditionalists have tried to have it both ways—blaming the child for immorality while at the same time using praise and punishment as if he or she could not really understand morality. There is even some hint that we are becoming aware of how we trap our children. We do discuss the "rights of children" and are developing legal protections for children's interests. We have not, however, done very much serious thinking about the consequences that would follow a demonstration of childhood's moral incompetence.

Obviously the debate is not put in such extreme terms, since all sides presume—a presumption that also needs examination—the benevolence of parents and teachers. Instead, the issue has been framed as one concerning the accessibility of certain kinds of ideas and certain kinds of thinking to students at different moments in their lives. Furthermore, the rigidity of cognitive and moral development ideas is softened in practice by the experience of the classroom. Thus, as "just community" experiments have been undertaken and as the use of dilemmas has shifted from the psychology laboratory to the classroom discussion, a good deal of sensitivity to student variability and plasticity has appeared.[17]

Stage notions also give us a misleading sense of security, which is one reason why we adopt them so readily. We are told that later stages must follow and incorporate prior stages, that the order is invariant—we must go through the first to get to the second, and so on—and that the process is hooked up to chronological age in some general way. At the same time, later moral stages are not only more inclusive but also morally better because more inclusive; that is, maturity shifts from a descriptive to a normative notion. Thus, we not only reach a point of being able to think in morally principled ways (stages 5 and 6 in Kohlberg's scheme), but "principled thinking" is morally preferable to "conventional thinking" (stages 3 and 4). Since principled thinking is paradigmatically philosophic, it follows that philosophic reflection—the fifth curriculum—is only available very late in a student's career and even then not for all students.

Such views appeal to our intuitions about readiness. For example, a recent popular text, David Elkind's *The Hurried Child*, was obviously summing up Piagetian ideas:

Much of our thinking is also symbolic, so that although children think, it is not until adolescence and the appearance of formal operations that young people think about thinking. It is at this time that words symbolize thought products and activities begin to appear in young people's vocabulary. Teen-agers, in contrast to children, begin to talk about what they "believe" and "value" and about "faith" and "motives." Thinking about their own and other people's thinking is a unique achievement of adolescent mental operations.[18]

We are also told that most people will never get beyond conventional thinking. Again, our ordinary experience is appealed to. It follows that principled morality and philosophic thought remain permanently closed off to most people. A moral hierarchy and a view that all thinking is of one kind have been embedded in a psychological theory without sufficient critical examination.[19]

Were "stages" only a metaphor for the readiness of a child, it would serve as a useful caution against moralism and as a guide to classroom observation. However, readiness has been transformed into a psychobiological hypothesis and an unconfessed determinism has been imported into our thinking. Thus, Piaget wrote:

If we examine the intellectual development of the individual or of the whole of humanity [*sic*], we shall find that the human spirit goes through a certain number of stages, each different from the other, but such that during each, the mind believes itself to be apprehending an external reality that is independent of the thinking subject. The content of this reality varies according to the stages: for the young child it is alive and permeated with finality, intentions, etc. whereas for the scientist, reality is characterized by physical determinism. But the ontological function, so to speak, remains identical: each in his own way thinks he has found the outer world in himself.[20]

These harsh—but unexposed—moral implications of development theory should not, however, blind us to its value when the necessary cautions have been observed. It is obvious that the child is not an adult, that there are brighter and duller students, that maturity is not simply a biological notion. It is also true that the notion of a "dilemma" conveys an essential moral insight—the availability of morally equivalent but different responses to moral questions, and, finally, it is true that development is a necessary feature of moral education, that it is foolish to expect 5-year-olds to work with the sophistication of 15-year-olds. As against an inherited moralism—the notion that a moral imperative can be applied willy-nilly to child and adult, to the educated and the uneducated, and so on—moral development in the hands of democratic and benevolent practitioners offers a humane and sensible perspective. However, benevolence and democracy evoke political and moral sources external to the psychology of development, and that has not been critically attended to.

By contrast, Philosophy for Children claims unequivocally to teach philosophic reasoning in elementary schools. It seems, in a sense, to be the polar response to moral development. With textbooks, teacher training programs, and independent measurements of classroom effectiveness, Philosophy for Children would appear to undercut the notion that reflective thinking is only available much later in a student's life.

The focus of Philosophy for Children, however, is on what are called "thinking skills," like analyzing, classifying, defining, inferring, and comparing. Thus, it is essentially a program in informal logic.

Many people find it hard to believe that philosophy could ever become an elementary school subject. They find the experimental results even harder to believe. In a year-long experiment conducted by the Educational Testing Service in Newark, New Jersey, highly significant improvements were recorded in reading, mathematics, and creative reasoning. . . . ETS conducted another experiment in 1980–81 involving over 2000 middle school students, using a highly sensitive test of formal and informal reasoning . . . pre and post-test scores showed that the experimental group's gain was 80% greater than the gain of the control group. . . . What makes philosophy so interesting to children? . . . [I]ts emphasis on meanings rather than on isolated facts; its emphasis on thinking rather than on mere memorizing; its stress on taking up issues which matter to the children themselves, rather than those primarily relevant only to the adult world; the many ways in which it helps children find reasons to support their personal views; and its contention that reasoning and concept development are best fostered by classroom dialogue. . . . Philosophy is an exceptional thinking skills program.[21]

Clearly, the reported success of Philosophy for Children places great weight on test scores and infers that the improvement of reading and mathematics test scores—certainly a worthwhile but still a narrow achievement—is an index of improvement in reading and mathematics themselves. This, in turn, is taken as an index of improvement in thinking skills, which in turn is equivalent to doing philosophy. This chain of inferences, however, needs defense, particularly since its image of philosophy promotes logic to the center stage of the philosophic enterprise and tends to underplay aesthetics, metaphysics, and even ethics. The program is heavily influenced by what is doable with large numbers of students in the elementary classroom. Nothing in development theory, by the way, precludes the notion that thinking skills are available to the young child. Thinking skills may be sequentially developed too, adequacy and complexity come with experience, and so on. The development that is recognized by Philosophy for Children is manifest in its own textbooks, which are grade-specific. A justification of the latter would lead to readiness and go easily down the "slippery slope" of stage rigidities. The formalism of moral development is matched by an equivalent formalism in the notion of thinking skills. Ironically, despite the frequent antagonism between those holding these views, they are one in their attack on moralism, in their recognition of maturation, in their reliance on reasoning, in their reference to an Aristotelian line of development in Western philosophy, and in their concern for explicit classroom activity on behalf of moral thinking.

If these best instances that seek to resolve the debate about development give us indeterminate results, what then can we say about the psychological and pedagogical practicability of the fifth curriculum? When in doubt, return to the classroom. There, despite the claims of developmentalists, we find that children do in fact reason abstractly, generally, and correctly. We find, too, that philosophy need not be limited to thinking skills and their derivatives, but we do not necessarily find reflection labelled as such or a large common language vocabulary available. Early childhood is characterized by a good deal of linguistic and symbolic inventiveness. The language is rich but unfamiliar to adults, and, because information is necessarily limited, we find children struggling for references. This often leads to creative fiction and to mixing information with fantasy. Only later is this imaginative richness replaced by more mundane reference.

For example, I observe a group of very young children in a kindergarten class.[22] As they "play house," they raise issues of fairness, say, in deciding how limited goods like cookies or crayons are to be shared. The philosopher in me recognizes issues of distributive justice. I catch on to their ability to see things as others see them—children take on the role of mother or of father, imitating what they have experienced, but they also improve on the roles, include self-criticism, criticism of how fellow students are enacting the roles, and even criticism of how their parents enact the roles. As a philosopher I might talk of objectivity and transcendance. Finally, they are quite articulate, albeit with a small and sometimes idiosyncratic vocabulary. They give their reasons, and reflect on what it means to do something better or worse. One child asks himself, "Why did I do that?" and another suggests alternatives. A third puts things in priority order from the point of view of what would be "fair." They are able to comment on motivation; for example, on why someone did what they ought not to have done. A philosopher calls it ethics and philosophical psychology. To be sure, the symbolic armory of young children is quite tangible—roles, cookies, crayons, costumes, and so forth—but these are symbols as well as things, and no less reflective for all that. Reflection also shows itself quite clearly in their discussions. They identify their "play" with a story they've heard or a picture they've drawn as well as with their own household or with media images. They are able, in other words, to develop a complex symbolic vocabulary and, led by their teacher, to work out methods of translation for themselves and between themselves and the adult world.

In another classroom, a third grade, as it happens, students are building up a legal and governmental system for themselves. They debate quite carefully about rights, about the distinctions between citizen and visitor and younger and older, about power and authority. They understand the limits of their classroom, the impact of the larger system—the school—on their ability to choose and to act. Indeed, when they find it onerous, they invoke the right of petition and file a grievance with the school principal. Of course, they only have a limited legal and social vocabulary, but they are engaged in reflection—"Why have rules at all?" and not simply "Why this rule rather than that?" Along the way, they talk about kinds of rules, and about who rules and why they do. Some raise issues of legitimacy: By what right is authority exercised at all?—there are some latent anarchists in the room—and the discussion is not limited only to pragmatic issues like limiting authority or finding ways of resolving conflicts of authority.

The classroom, in other words, challenges the categories with which we debate development, and thus in the doing, both dilemma discussions and Philosophy for Children point toward the fifth curriculum. Students are stimulated by dilemmas and by reasoning exercises. Typically they refuse to be limited by the protocols for discussing dilemmas or by the structured exercises of Philosophy for Children.[23] Unless held back by adults, they invent their own dilemmas and write their own stories, so it is not finally by curriculum alone that reflection is developed, nor does the classroom work itself out automatically. Much as children bring to the classroom the capacities for the fifth curriculum, those capacities can be either deadened or invigorated.

To do philosophy with a child, or with anyone else for that matter, is simply to reflect on a perplexity or a conceptual problem of a certain sort to see if one can remove the perplexity or solve the problem. Sometimes one succeeds, often one doesn't. Sometimes getting clearer about one thing only makes it obvious that one is dreadfully unclear about something else. . . . To do philosophy successfully with children requires that one rid oneself of all defensiveness. . . . [One] should simply enlist the child's help so that [both adult and child] . . . can try together to work out a satisfactory answer.[24]

We turn then to the art of teaching. The central figure in the drama of moral education comes on stage.

Notes

1. A thorough and useful discussion of parental modeling and parental standards was offered by Michael Schulman in an as yet unpublished paper, "Why Isn't There More Street Crime?" (University Seminar on Moral Education, at Columbia University, April 1987). See also Michael Schulman and Eva Mekler, *Bringing up a Moral Child* (Reading, Mass.: Addison-Wesley, 1985).

2. For example, see Lawrence Kohlberg, "The Moral Atmosphere of the School," in *The Hidden Curriculum and Moral Education*, ed. H. Giroux and D. Purpel (Berkeley, Calif.: McCutcheon, 1983), pp. 61–81.

3. Lawrence Kohlberg, unlike many who use his ideas, was quite aware that he was mixing normative and descriptive categories. He made his attempt explicit in "From Is to Ought: How to Commit the Naturalistic Fallacy and Get Away With It. . . ," in his *The Philosophy of Moral Development*, vol. 1 (San Francisco: Harper and Row, 1981), pp. 101–89.

4. Mark Weinstein in "Reason and the Child" (University Seminar on Moral Education, March 1987) writes,

For Kohlberg, the highest available level [of philosophical maturity] is epitomized in the work of Rawls. It is hard to see the justification of [this] claim. The Utilitarians, for example, were quite conscious of Kant as are contemporary teleologists. Deontological perspectives are not uncontroversial in philosophical thought. (p. 25)

5. Within three years of Rawls's *A Theory Of Justice* (Cambridge, Mass.: Harvard, 1971), Robert Nozick had published his alternative, *Anarchy, State, and Utopia* (New York: Basic Books, 1974), and Norman Daniels had collected some 14 critical essays from among many available in *Reading Rawls* (New York: Basic Books, 1974).

6. For an early, readable, and still insightful discussion of analytic philosophy, see A. J. Ayer, *Language, Truth, and Logic* 2d ed. (New York: Dover, 1936). For a criticism of reducing philosophy to language, see the brilliant and amusing essay by Ernest Gellner, *Words and Things* (Middlesex, England: Pelican, 1968). The controversy among philosophers continues. See Richard Bernstein, "Philosophical Rift: A Tale of Two Approaches," *New York Times*, December 29, 1987.

7. See Bernard Williams, *Ethics and the Limits of Philosophy* (Cambridge, Mass.: Harvard University Press, 1985), chapter 5.

8. Maxine Greene of Teachers College, Columbia, makes the point:

The concern of teacher educators must remain normative, critical, and even political—neither the colleges nor the schools can change the social order. Neither the colleges nor the schools can legislate democracy. But something can be done to empower teachers to reflect upon their own life situations, to speak out in their own ways about the lacks that must be repaired; the possibilities to be acted upon in the name of what they deem decent, humane, and just.

In *Landscapes of Learning* (New York: Teachers College Press, 1978), p. 71.

9. See Ravitch, "Where Have All the Classics gone?"

10. Paulo Friere, *Philosophy of the Oppressed* (New York: Seabury Press, 1973), p. 15.

11. See Marguerete K. Rivage-Seul, "Peace Education: Imagination and the Pedagogy of the Oppressed," *Harvard Educational Review* 57, no. 2 (May 1987): 153–69.

12. John Dewey, "Context and Thought," in *On Experience, Nature, and Freedom*, ed. Richard J. Bernstein, Indianapolis: Bobbs-Merrill, 1960, p. 107.

13. Gareth Matthews, *Philosophy and the Young Child*, Cambridge, Mass.: Harvard University Press, 1984, p. 73.

14. Christian Bay, "Peace and Critical Political Knowledge as Human Rights," *Political Theory*, 8, no. 3 (Summer 1980): 293-318.

15. See Diane Ravitch, "Tot Sociology," including a discussion of grade school history and what has happened to it, in *The American Scholar* 56, no. 3 (Summer 1987): 343.

16. For one view, see the brief but cogent commentary of Richard S. Peters, "Why Doesn't Lawrence Kohlberg Do his Homework?" reprinted from *Phi Delta Kappan* (June 1975) in *Moral Education . . . It Comes with the Territory*, ed. D. Purpel and K. Ryan, (Berkeley, Calif.: McCutchan Publishing, 1976), pp. 288-90.

17. I cannot cite text for this comment. I can, however, report my own observations and my conversations with Lawrence Kohlberg, Thomas Lickona, James Rest, and with teachers and consultants active in two current projects in New York City at Roosevelt High School and at the Bronx High School of Science. These conversations reflect a sense of openness that is strikingly absent from the protocols and descriptions of the assessment of dilemma responses in research. Classroom and laboratory have not as yet, however, managed to stimulate each other sufficiently.

Similarly, Philosophy for Children has missed out on its homework. For example, the use of quantitative testing instruments as indices of philosophic instruction seems, to say the least, to raise questions that cannot be fudged about the relationships of quantity and quality. Further, the assimilation of thinking skills to thinking needs exploration; and, finally, the introduction of discussion in classrooms—typically overcrowded public-school classrooms characterized by traditional teacher-centered methods—may well produce good results because of a "Hawthorne effect," the effect of attention itself.

Both moral development and Philosophy for Children are useful and exciting. Perhaps this is one more instance where an apparent eclecticism has rational justification.

18. David Elkind, *The Hurried Child* (Reading, Mass.: Addison-Wesley, 1981), p. 111.

19. For a more complex view of "thinking," see Howard Gardner, *Frames of Mind: The Theory of Multiple Intelligences* (New York: Basic Books, 1983).

20. Jean Piaget, "The Child's Conception of Physical Causality," 1927, in *The Essential Piaget*, ed. H. E. Gruber and J. J. Voneche (New York: Basic Books, 1977), p. 128.

21. Institute for the Advancement of Philosophy for Children, *Philosophy for Children, 1987* (Montclair, New Jersey, 1987), pp. 53 and S4.

22. These are not single or singular examples. They reflect my own observations together with comments from many teachers.

23. In the classroom and in talks with teachers I have been impressed with the need of students for generating their own dilemmas once introduced to the notion. Typically, they elicit them from their own experience in school or at home, from current events, and so on. Similarly, when we have tried it with students accustomed to discussion and a rich bibliography, we have found that both teachers and students refused to restrict their readings to the structured texts published by the Institute for the Advancement of Philosophy for Children. Typically, we have seen the development of readings from an abundant and aesthetically satisfying literature for children.

24. Gareth Matthews, *Philosophy and the Young Child* (Cambridge, Mass.: Harvard University Press, 1980), pp. 83–85.

7

Character and Characters: Voices in the Classroom

The classroom is a mixture of laughter and sobriety. We teachers confess this double reality in our daily lives and when we are not performing political theater at budget time or at a PTA meeting. As students, we remember the buffoon and the brain, the athlete and the sex symbol. We remember our teachers as clowns and as heroes, and at times as bores. We remember moments of sadness, and of high and low comedy, and we remember the names and faces. Thus we go to class reunions, or greet an old school friend accidentally met with warmth and affection. To the observer, every reunion is like every other; to the participant, it is unique. We remember, too, that we learned almost in spite of ourselves, and that we didn't learn by going neatly from lesson to lesson. After the fact, in review sessions and on examinations, the classroom appeared—but only appeared—ordered and orderly.

All of this is by way of saying that theater is an apt metaphor for schooling. The teacher knows it; he or she is "on" every minute, which is why good teaching is so exhausting. Students need to become actors too or the classroom fails. That is why good learning is exhausting, too. Sadly, the language of educational reform, using an industrial metaphor like "productivity" or a political metaphor like "relevance," misses the point. It ignores the rhythm and tempo, the texture, of an effective classroom.

The classroom unfolds as it plays. To be sure, subjects like language, history, arithmetic, and science—ironically, especially the latter—seem to limit our adventurousness, although good teaching produces surprises everywhere. In these subjects, we think that we already know what we will find, yet each class is different, and there are discoveries enough even in teaching the so-called basics.

Images from theater are particularly applicable to moral education. Its classroom is a setting of events and personalities. Human relationships as they happen to students and teachers are its primary substance. Even where the material seems abstract—a short story, a dilemma, a logical analysis—the unspoken reference is to those who are present. These relationships are in play in every classroom, but they are only incidental to the argument of history, mathematics, or literature. When we try to choreograph moral education too strictly— to teach lessons and rules as we teach them in other subjects—we are ineffective and clumsy. Just as "rule-directed" behavior works where no moral problem is posed, so "rule-directed" moral education works where no education is needed. It fails to capture the student's interest because no interesting question is posed.

The opening act of moral education begins with the tensions of the interesting situation. Where it counts, we do not face clear choices between good and evil. Our principles are muddied by feelings, histories, and relationships. The individuality of persons and the uniqueness of events turn precedents into novelties. We might wish it were otherwise. However, when we do find our ethics neatly packaged, as in a "morality play" we are easily bored. To be sure, some stories with a "moral," for example, "David and Goliath" or "Daniel in the Lion's Den," capture us as adventures or because they have interesting characters. However, the "moral" is more likely to be an adult interest; the action is the child's. Of course, we inflict "Sunday School" lessons on our children because it's "good for them," but we show by our absence that we think it is only good for them and not for us. They, of course, do not agree.

Now this is not just a commentary on human obstinacy or on the fact that we find evil more interesting than good. The play of heroism and villainy connects to our own moral reality. Within us are the conflicts, the temptations, the lapses, the choices between this good or that and between lesser and greater evils. Our neighbors have the same conflicts, although we wear masks that hide us from each other and even from ourselves. Moral education then is a mystery story as well as a farce. It develops with the exposure of pretention.

A language of roles, conflicts, and masks, of character and story, fits quite naturally with our moral experience. We resonate to moral drama, feel the "pity and terror" that for Aristotle led through tragedy to catharsis. We are morally engaged. Theater thus has a double sanction as a metaphor for moral education: it is natural to the subject matter and it is natural to effective teaching.

II

The scene opens when good and evil turn into a problem.[1] We feel uncomfortable, dislocated. At first we try practical solutions, adjustments, compromises—we try to accommodate to inherited wisdom, but if the dissonance remains and the discomfort persists, we find that we need a different attention. For example, we come up against a situation that does not allow for the either/or of truth telling. At one moment, honesty is fitting, yet at the next it is only priggish or even destructive; or perhaps the community ceases to command our loyalty and resistance replaces cooperation. Facing these conflicts, we wonder about ourselves too and about those whom we trust. The dislocation enlarges.

For example, we may react to shifts in power or to economic troubles, but we do not readily accept the fact that changes in us and in the world ask for changes in morality. Virtue is, we have been told, unchanging, so a gap opens between moral reality and other realities. We become survivors in practice and moralists in rhetoric. At the same time, we take our practice and our morals seriously. We are thus distanced from ourselves, but we don't know why. Our discomfort increases even more. We become impatient, angry, and anxious. Even if the changes are not for the worse—perhaps we benefit from a shift in power—the gap remains, although muted by undeserved satisfaction. Guilt joins our other discomforts, so the moral scene accrues an emotional charge too, and is latent with feelings, fears, and hopes. However, the process of dislocation is not merely negative. In fact, as discomfort grows, indifference dies. We are ready to learn. The classroom, in other words, needs confusion, pain, discomfort—then our interest and our interests will be at stake.

We need not wait upon events. Happenings can be induced and then converted into curriculum. Thus a teacher may seize upon an event—a quarrel between two students, a violation of school rules, a death in the family, a community crisis—or may use a story, a dilema, or a play to create one. Above all, a teacher knows how to listen.

An ethical problem that third graders often bring up themselves is that of the wish for revenge. . . . Sometimes, the discussion of this issue can be very moving and sometimes very practical. Third graders will say, quite emotionally, "I know that I *shouldn't* really hurt the other person back, but I know that I *would* really try to hurt him. . . ." Once a boy said, "If I didn't get him back, I know it would just eat at me and eat at me inside until I couldn't stand it any more!" Another boy had a practical suggestion: "When I get mad at someone like that, I write his name and some bad stuff on a piece of paper, and I keep doing that for a few days, and then finally I just crumble the piece of paper all up. The person never knows but I feel better."[2]

Teachers turn events into the stuff of moral education, but we cannot preach a sermon. Instead, the morally interesting situation plays out naturally in a dialogue. That is our genre, our kind of theater. Unfortunately, "dialogue" has become a cliche, and even a verb. Indeed, we use the word just about any time we choose to talk instead of fight. However, a dialogue is not simply talk, it has its cast of characters and its pattern of encounters and oppositions.

In all drama we identify with the characters. What happens to them is taken as real and is felt as real. The characters also take on a life of their own, and are not mere puppets, but in most drama there is still a distance between us and the stage, a proscenium and a curtain. We leave the theater after the play concludes, moved, enlightened, and pensive. However, the play does conclude; the history, English, or science lesson does end.

In a dialogue we are the characters; we are on stage, and the play does not conclude. At the close of a lesson, our knowledge will not be as it was—at the close of a dialogue we will not be as we were. We do not simply exchange views or opinions as in a discussion, nor do we act out a script as in a standard lesson. In a dialogue, the moral development of persons and ideas together is a permanent subtext. The characters are both unique and representative, their participation is existential and conceptual. As with all drama, a dialogue is a moral experience, but in it we do not simply talk about experiences as in a good discussion or witness experiences as in a good play. In doing moral education, a teacher is not a discussion leader, an instructor, or a drama coach. A student does not simply receive, observe, or absorb.

At the same time, a dialogue is not moral experience in the world. It stands to one side as an exploration, an attempt to fit form and reflection. It asks for a suspension of judgement while a play asks for a suspension of belief. It asks for a renewal of alternatives while a discussion looks toward closure. In a dialogue we always ask another question, and questions are everywhere. Teachers find them in history or art, in current events, in an anecdote or a classroom quarrel. A dialogue develops as a reflection on what has occurred, and it develops unpredictably. It is an experience that is had but it also informs the rest of the experience we have. In other words, a dialogue is the form taken by the fifth curriculum.

In a dialogue, teachers discover the Socratic role. Thus they are both players in and creators of a dialogue. Both positions are held at the same time. We come upon our vocational ideal: the teacher as "midwife" to ideas, as present to the creation and recreation of persons. Unfortunately, this peculiar kind of self-consciousness, certainly not without its own difficulty, is burdened by an image of Socrates that is freighted with mythic perfections. Legend has joined symbolism in an idealized portrait, helped no doubt by translators enamored of King James English and by religionists eager to capture a "pagan" hero as their own. Thus we carry a picture of Socrates as a sort of pre-Christian Christian martyr. That turns Socrates into an icon. The classroom reality is different and accessible to all of us.

Of course, Socrates comes to us in the biased reports of his student, Plato.[3] Other images are less flattering—the figure of sophistry and satire in Aristophanes, for example. Even Plato tells of a character who was annoying, persistent, patronizing, satirizing, contradicting, impractical—always running after an interesting idea, neglecting his family, and jealous of fellow teachers. It is this ambivalent image that is more like ourselves and that serves us as the original figure of moral inquiry and moral commitment. Finally, it is the Socratic figure engaged in a dialogue who is a guide to all future moral education.

Such . . . absence of conclusion illustrates the attitude peculiar to Socrates among all the great teachers of the world. He will not do their thinking for the men who come to him, neither in matters small nor great. In the *Cratylus* where the young man and his friends approach him with a question about language and how names are formed, all the satisfaction they get is: "If I had not been a poor man, I might have heard the fifty drachma course of the great Prodicus which is a complete education in grammar and language . . . and then I should have been able . . . to answer your question. But . . . I have only heard the single drachma course and therefore I do not know the truth about such matters. Still I will gladly assist you in the investigation of them." . . . [T]he investigation ends with "This may be true, Cratylus, but it is also very likely to be untrue; and therefore I would not have you be too easily persuaded. . . . Reflect well for you are young and of an age to learn. And when you have found the truth, come and tell me." To which the young man answers—he must have been very young—"I will do as you say, Socrates."[4]

Socrates comes to us with a teacher's contradictions—patient and preaching, humble and arrogant, kindly and stiff-necked. Even when called to defend his life—in Plato's *Apology*—there is humor and poignancy, irony and anger, realism and abstraction, and, above all, talk. The source of all future philosophic reflection, Socrates is a figure of moral drama. He does not explain, but participates in explanation. Unfortunately, a later Platonism turned Socratic insight into abstract principle, put the ideal into another world, and made moral teaching an alien activity.

Back among us, we can yet find the theme struck by the Socratic figure: reflection arises within moral biography and out of its conflicts. For example, that most puzzling and revealing of Socratic claims makes sense only in a dialogue: "I know that I know nothing," is paradoxical and ironic. If Socrates knows "nothing," then who can be said to "know" anything? If Socrates can say the truthfully false and the falsely true, then who can be found to speak the truth? His claim is also a counterclaim, so it is in fact no claim at all. However, it is framed as a statement of experience and not as an abstract proposition. Contradiction is felt and had, and this motivates the interplay of the characters in a dialogue.

In conversation about good and evil, we are always tempted to open with accepted wisdom, saying what is morally so and not so. Unfortunately, this wisdom turns out to be less than helpful as it is complicated by contradiction, so we try to find out what our statements mean. The first move of a dialogue is definitional. A well-placed question reveals our confusions about meanings. For example, we ask, "What is justice?" in Plato's *Republic* and we are "answered" with inconsistent alternatives. At the same time, we are in love with our own ideas, so we cannot tolerate those who contradict us. At first, therefore, we do not listen to them; we cannot even hear them. Typically, we speak louder and slower, become more insistent, and try to strengthen our case by repeating our answers as if repetition could capture the truth by storm. The teacher annoys us by not taking sides, and shows by listening that he or she expects us to listen. Soon we are confused and find ourselves unable to choose between the competing voices. Our repetitions become restatements. The moral vocabulary enlarges but, since no synonym is ever exact, restatements begin to change what we are saying. At first we do not realize it. We are angry and impatient.

Meanwhile, our fellow students are up to the same thing. Events, which are introduced as illustration and as argument, only increase the contradiction, because events are never seen in only one way. Our moral language is inadequate to events. It seems always to be behind things, and does not resolve or clarify the issues. The teacher calls attention to this inadequacy. More definition follows. The listener in us separates from the speaker in us, but is not yet freed to speak and admit the possibilities of good sense in the other. More than one conversation goes on in us as a dialogue develops. The act of saying itself changes the event and its setting, and so we have to re-say.

At first we do not know any of this. We simply take turns talking at each other. We describe, we expound, we explain, we preach, we demand, we justify, and we argue. The teacher does not let us forget that our explanations are met by the convincing explanations of others. We say more. Our opponents do the same. Proposal begets counterproposal. The teacher—with a word, an interjection—encourages speaking by making spaces for others to speak. Finally we hear our own confession; we know that we do not know, and knowing begins.

Teachers strip away our secured wisdom for the sake of constructive ignorance. The task is critical and surely negative. Scepticism transforms us and our ideas again and again, but the transformation is never completed. There is always a next moment in biography— which is why the Greeks had it right when they said, "Call no man happy until he is dead"—and why there is always a next question in the classroom. The Socratic art is also quite modern—or perhaps today is a reprise of all our yesterdays. We find Socratic similarities, for example, in John Dewey's notion of "reconstruction," and he was surely no Platonist. Critical inquiry, constructive ignorance, is a common theme of science, democracy, and schooling.

A dialogue takes form as the interplay of oppositions and of opponents. When effective, it reaches student and teacher; no one will leave unchanged. Its setting—the language and the landscape—is not merely ornamental. Dialogue can take place in Athens but not in Sparta, in the academy but not in the pulpit. Like the moral situation, the moral drama begins in the middle of things—a question, a puzzle, a problem thrown up or called up out of experience—and ends in the middle of things. We pause from time to time, but we do not conclude. Interesting questions will be reopened and, as we are further along, will be reopened again, but differently.

When we think of moral ideas as dramatic themes, then we need not treat moral philosophy as established truth and moral education as initiation into it. Moral history, after all, is point and counterpoint. The great themes—justice, love, and truth—are carried by people and events in all their mixture. We can also stop telling moral lies to each other. We need not force our students to choose sides or to become advocates where we know that advocacy is a mistake. There will be time and space enough for partisanship, but not in school, not in the dialogue.

In a debate one submits one's best thinking and defends it against challenges to show that it is right; in a dialogue one submits one's best thinking knowing that other people's reflections will help improve it rather than destroy it. . . . A debate is oppositional—two sides oppose each other and attempt to prove each other wrong; a dialogue is collaborative—two or more sides work toward common understanding.

Debate defends assumptions as truth; dialogue reveals assumptions for re-evaluation.

Debate creates . . . a determination to be right; dialogue creates an . . . openness to being wrong and an openness to learning.[5]

A dialogue is also an entertainment. We fool around with moral ideas, and this is not just a pedagogical trick or a gimmick for capturing the student's interest. Philosophy, after all, is the discipline of reflective exploration; that is, intellectual "fooling around." Of course, we can force our students to repeat "Virtue is its own reward," by using our authority. Thereby we close our moral education with a motto. However, we want to stir up questions, or more likely, we can't suppress questions, so we go to work even on a motto:

What do we mean by reward? Do we mean fame, success, money, recognition, pleasure? Do we know where virtue was unrewarding? . . . or where it was unrewarded? What do we mean by vice? Isn't vice often preferred? If something is preferred, is it preferrable? . . .

Often the questions we're used to asking are like the exercises found at the end of chapters in a textbook. They are nonquestions, and they will not do. Other questions are meant for contemplation, and they will not do either. Then, however, there are interesting questions, so, we need to listen to each other, and for that, we must learn to keep still. The teacher demonstrates the uses of silence by stepping back after asking a question, by letting others do the talking, then using another question and yet another, forcing talk toward hesitation and reflection.

Keeping silent is another essential possibility of discourse, and it has the same existential foundation. In talking with one another, the person who keeps silent can "make one understand". . . and he can do so more authentically than the person who is never short of words. Speaking at length about something does not offer the slightest guarantee that thereby understanding is advanced. On the contrary, talking extensively about something covers it up and brings what is understood to a sham clarity—the unintelligibility of the trivial. But to keep silent does not mean to be dumb. On the contrary, if a man is dumb, he still has a tendency to "speak." Such a person has not proved that he can keep silence; indeed he entirely lacks the possibility of proving anything of the sort. And the person who is accustomed by nature to speak little is no better able to show that he is keeping silent or that he is the sort of person who can do so. . . . Keeping silent authentically is possible only in genuine discoursing.[6]

There are questions that will strike us as interesting and others that are arid, but we don't know which is which until we try them. This accounts for the stumbling, hesitant quality of a dialogue. Knowing the members of the cast—ourselves and our students—helps, but we are changing too, so what we knew of each other when we began will become misleading as we proceed. The chance of error increases just because we mistake each other, but then, mistakes become further occasions for the dialogue. The Socratic art needs patience with a process that invites false starts and dead ends.

Of course, classrooms and teachers vary. We know that the "same" material may or may not work with different groups of students, or on different days, or when it is gloomy or sunny, or if the class comes early or late in the day. Ordinarily we treat these as incidental conditions. We fight for a better schedule, try to "balance" the makeup of our classes, or look for a chance to teach brighter students. In a dialogue, however, we cannot know in advance which differences are incidental and which are morally relevant. We get a clue when a question excites a response, but by then, a dialogue has begun. We get a clue from our own responses too; from what touches us, excites us, interests us. Again, however, this is not known in advance, so we never put old questions away, because they have a way of becoming new again. We cannot forecast distinctions between the important and the unimportant or the relevant and the irrelevant. In other forms of inquiry, these distinctions set the task, for example, in the way in which a researcher formulates a hypothesis or a policy-maker sets priorities. Such distinctions, however, become part of the dialogue itself when we probe their reasons and are asked to justify our judgements of attentiveness or priority.

Teachers mistake their students when they complain that students "ought" to be interested or that something is "important." Teaching is always tempted toward preaching. In a dialogue, however, we ask why the disparity of interests or the varied interests exist. In finding out, we come upon moral tensions; for example, by recognizing the opposition between my interests and yours.

We find that dialogue is accessible by doing it and not by talking about it. We can all be apprentices to Socrates. For example, a teacher of ten-year-olds wrote,

One of the first . . . concepts that the social studies teacher can help young people to grasp is that information can be "true" without being "the truth.". . .

I began this year by putting a time line on the board and asking what at first seemed a very simple question: "When should a study of American history begin?"

Answers varied: "Columbus," "Pilgrims," "Vikings," "Indians."

We could not find a clear consensus. "How can this be?" I asked. "We're going to spend a year studying American history and we can't even agree on when it begins."

We brought out five textbooks of American history. No luck: five books, four different beginnings.

"Now what?" I asked. Silence.

Finally, someone said, "You just have to make a choice."

"Based on what?" I asked. "Should we draw lots, flip coins?" Silence.

When in doubt, ask more questions. What questions could we ask about the five different textbooks? . . .

Someone asked: "*Why* do they begin at different times?"

Someone conjectured that it makes sense to begin with the Indians since they were there first. "Excellent," we replied.

"But what about the books which *don't* begin with the Indians, or only when they met Columbus? *Why* did they choose not to?"

Someone ventured the idea that maybe the author didn't think the Indians were important. "You mean in his *opinion* the Indians weren't important?" we asked.

"But is history fact or opinions?"

We then talked about the nature of this thing called history and how it is not just a collection of facts but is very much influenced by opinions and assumptions; that depending on what source you read, you may very well get different impressions.[7]

III

A dialogue is a pattern of encounters. At first, we only hear the voices of the actual participants. They have proper names. We listen again. Now, we hear recurring voices too, echoes of other dialogues, and even echoes of universal themes. As a dialogue develops, these are integrated, building on what went before. In the beginning, we meet around a particular moment and its conflict. Our moral interest is stirred. For example, we are in Athens. Socrates is accused of subverting the faith and morals of the young and will be on trial for his life. He meets Euthyphro, a religious scholar, who reports that he is about to accuse his father of manslaughter. That, Euthyphro claims, is what the gods would wish him to do. Socrates praises this model of piety and asks for help in preparing his defense. Corrupting the youth is also an issue of piety. Euthyphro misses the irony of the situation; he is a very serious man as befits a theologian, so he is quick to oblige. Socrates asks questions, and then asks more questions. Euthyphro grows more confused in thought—how many kinds of piety are there?—and more certain in speech.

There are hidden questions too; parallel dialogues are going on at the same time. Socrates encounters himself as well as Euthyphro, although this will appear more clearly in the sequel—in Plato's *Crito* and *Phaedo*. We are also present. We have our own encounters and recall our own certainties. Connections appear between autobiography and biography, between biography and principle. We are transformed from audience into actors. Euthyphro alone seems to be untouched. He repeats himself, is driven into logical corners—he is a constant reminder of our starting point, alternately annoyed, condescending, curious, uncomfortable, sure, and puzzled. Even as he rehearses the conventional wisdom, he struggles with reason and finds it intolerable. The trial of Socrates is, as it were, over in the prologue, and it has yet to happen.

We will revisit Athens many times. Perhaps we start again by thinking ourselves into the place of Euthyphro's father or the murdered slave, or we ask if matters might be different were the characters women and not men. A dialogue expects us to be in many places and to explore many places, but how would our moral ideas change if our places changed? A dialogue probes this question of position and generality, of situation and universal, over and over again. *Euthyphro* closes on a final irony—we continue walking together, Socrates the accused and Euthyphro to accuse. The situation seems not to have changed at all; reason, or so the message might be read, seems helpless before events. That, of course, is the opening for another dialogue.

Other dialogues and other encounters follow, bringing new questions and familiar patterns. "What is justice?" We meet the counterclaims of power and reason in the *Republic*. "What is love?" We explore its varieties in the *Symposium*. "What is knowledge?" We listen as the teacher and the slave talk in the *Meno*. Death encounters survival and loyalty encounters prudence in the *Crito* and the *Phaedo*.[8]

A dialogue begins in the particulars. The players bring their histories with them. Socrates is the teacher of Athens; Alcibiades is the soldier of Athens.[9] However, soon we will hear other voices too, and they will be representative of universal themes, not just of particular concerns and moments. If these universal voices did not appear, we might be interested only as we are interested in gossip: will Socrates live or die, or will Euthyphro really face his father in court? We would remain an audience, enjoying or criticizing the play and the players. No doubt, we would laugh or cry—but the curtain would come down. We do not, however, depart from a dialogue. We carry it on after we leave, peopling our own imaginations as in revery or daydreaming.

In a dialogue, we hear these representative voices speaking through one of the participants. A dialogue embeds moral law or ethical principle in a character or characters, for example, as the gods play a role in drama or as teachers inter-weave their personality with their calling. The characters develop by bringing into unity the representative and the unique; they are not simply vehicles for eternal and changeless abstractions. Thus, a dialogue is a moral exhibition. It shows us encountering particular moral questions as we experience them. At the same time, it shows these questions to be instances of moral questions that have been asked before and that will be asked again; and finally, it shows how our particular moment is at the same time a part of history, both unique for what it is and connected to other unique moments to form a pattern.

When we separate what was had by others in the past, what is had by us in the present, and what is to be had by others yet to come, we trap ourselves into judgements of other people while giving ourselves moral alibis. We can always find excuses for ourselves in our experience. Its details and its complexities are rich with possibilities for explaining away our faults and failures. At the same time, we separate our own experience from the moral process by thinking of moral problems through the abstracted language of principle. We strip away the details and connect the instance and the principled judgement as question and response in a moral routine. For example, when we are able to call something a "lie" and someone a "liar," we think we have laid the moral problem to rest. However, the language of principle seldom reaches our own problem, which always remains an exception. That language of principle really reaches only to someone else's acts and motives. To ourselves, we are never instances. We know—or think we do—why we did what we did; we have our own explanations, but they are peculiar to us. In a dialogue, the person with his or her particular experience is a legitimate participant and is not silenced, but he or she is forced to account for himself or herself by reference beyond the personal experience alone. Excuses and explanations are not moral justifications. The morally interesting situation cannot be resolved by apology or abstraction.

IV

In the beginning, the players all talk at once. We listen in. Many questions occur to us but we enter only where we find our students. Our first questions are to their problems, but our thought is not only of their problems. Our task, after all, is not therapy. Our project is to move from monologue to dialogue, to connect the autobiographical to the conceptual.

Thus teachers listen for possible connections that can lead people out of the natural concern for themselves alone. A syntax emerges in the language of every dialogue that shapes its moves. In the claim and counterclaim of the opening, a "first person" is heard, a predialogue in which I encounter myself. The background question is one of identity, "Who am I, where am I going, and what is happening to me?" Others are present but I do not yet address them; I'm talking to myself. Thus Dante begins *The Divine Comedy* "midway in the course of my life"—but he is writing in the presence of others and is not simply writing a diary or a private chronology. A high-school senior encounters an unexpected career choice. Parents divorce and a child is caught up in a question of loyalties. A hero is found taking drugs and a model becomes problematic, or, finally, I disappoint myself. In a dialogue I cannot close these matters in to myself; I expose them and am exposed. Soon, therefore, I meet other "I's," and even detect the hint of a representative "I." I come across continuities, reminders of others in what seemed only autobiography, only my problem.

This encounter with the first person seems to ask a question of meaning, but the meanings sought are still personal. "What does this mean to me?" For a moment, I find answers that satisfy me, but as I state the answers, I discover new questions. When I fail to discover new questions, others pose them for me and to me. I try to end the discomfort of this interrogation by asserting that "Justice is. . . ." or that "Love is. . . ." However, I find out that finding meanings is not a schoolboy's exercise. In a dialogue, I cannot turn to a dictionary. Others are all around me, and I encounter them. They make demands and I must attend. Even when I appear satisfied and ignore the others, I do not rest. My mind is filled with questions that do not go away. I talk to myself as we all do when unable to sleep. I say to myself, "What if. . . ." or "If only I had. . . ." The others find their way into my head, so to speak. If the matter is morally interesting, doubt persists. I return over and over again in a kind of moral revery. For the teenager facing military conscription, loyalty and service cease to be abstract moral notions. For the man or woman about to marry, promise giving is not simply the notion of contract. For the child-challenging parent or teacher, integrity and obedience are no longer virtues to be recited. I worry the question and it worries me. Above all, it does not go away.

However, a dialogue is not a "confession." The first person does not speak alone. In their "confessions," Augustine, Rousseau, and Newman all end, as it were, in self-discovery. Their achievement is self-revelation—and we are not expected to answer. As a dialogue develops, however, we hear other voices. A "third person" offers a "rule" or a "norm." The characters take turns as spokespersons for "society," the "state," or the "law," using the impersonal voice that begins sentences with "it" or "they." The third person proclaims the wisdom of the polis or the universe. Thus, Job's "comforters" speak in the voice of a "third person." In a school, we hear abstract but potent beings like "the faculty," "the parent body," "the administration," or, more rarely, "the students." For the third person there is no moral puzzlement and no revery. There are only questions of clarification and enforcement. We are forced into an admission of violation, ignorance, or guilt. We hear the demands of legitimacy and authority, and we have moved from confession to confrontation. Teachers nurture this meeting, since the first person is always tempted to give itself excuses or to escape into confession, and the third person is always tempted to righteousness.

It is the third person that announces the great virtues like justice and truth, and it is the third person that also claims moral objectivity. Thus we hear that the law knows neither person nor favor, and we say, "Justice is blind." The third person thus appears at a moral distance. Its tone and language is quite formal and so, paradoxically, it is familiar, even comforting. It has, as we also say, no self-interest but only the public interest as its reason for being. Hence, we feel a certain awe in its presence, yet it cannot know us in our particularity, and that is its failure when we confront moral problems. The morally interesting situation appears in an environment of passions too, of subjects and not just of objects. Unlike moral codes and principles—for example, legal commentaries and ethics texts—a morally interesting situation is never only the application of rules to cases. Thus the third person is also felt as alien and alienating.

However, a dialogue is not a power struggle. To leave first and third person alone in conflict would only result in acquiescence or revolt as is often the case in the world of action.[10] The encounter would circle around issues of legitimacy, for example, "May society rightly expect obedience of me?" and issues of autonomy, such as, "May I be a conscientious objector?" Another voice is needed. To become a dialogue, the encounter is mediated by a "second person."

The second person addresses us as "thou" and speaks in the language of the lower. Its voice emerges from tribe, family, or friendship. It is intimacy embodied, neither alien nor ego. It puts in context the autobiographical features of self and the normative features of society.[11] The second person is thus the natural voice of the "teacher" in moral education, and perhaps in all education. In other words, we have an inherent bias, a love, for our students. At the same time, we are not parents or elders, and we are critics. The second person is thus problematic for us. We need to be inside the dialogue to be effective. We too will speak in our own voice. We too will be transformed; but then, we are easily trapped into mere participation. We move outside to avoid this trap but thus are reduced to mere observation, and that is inadequate too. Hence, teachers are made anxious by dialogue because our role is flickering and ambivalent, so we try to escape by becoming disciplinarians or academic authorities. We become the teacher as alien. We speak in the language of the profession—the teacher as third person—and not the calling. From time to time, a reversal occurs and teachers try to be just like their students. We "hang around," wear student costume, and use student language. We "identify" with our students and fail once more.

The second person muddies the moral waters by saying that neither the self-interest of the first person nor the objectivity of the third person will do. We cannot simply choose between objectivity and needs; for example, between justice and caring.[12] The second person carries communal and traditional values into the encounter. Its voice is a reminder that the moral situation needs to take account of persons while not allowing individuality to deteriorate into moral alibi. Justice encounters coordinate values like kindness and love. The individual moves beyond self-interest to take account of known others such as family members and unknown others such as fellow citizens. The outcome is no longer a singular assertion of collective over individual rights. The love of parent for child, of teacher for student, is expressed in this mediation between "I" and "they." At the same time, the second person also develops. Communal values overcome a natural chauvinism—once there were "Greeks and barbarians"—and admit the legitimacy of other communities. The tribe comes to wider meanings as children or women become persons.

In the syntax of a dialogue, the three voices address each other, providing a pattern for moral discourse. Particular voices blend with representative ones. Through the latter, dialogues connect to each other across time and culture, so Socrates is not a stranger in the present. We might, for example, reflect on how the pattern reappears in a recent discussion with students looking at the moral effects of TV. When we note the presence and yet the ineffectiveness of the third person, we also see that a dialogue can also be an instrument of moral diagnosis.

When I took this a step further and asked the class if it would dump chemicals into a town sewer system or sell illegal drugs in order to save a failing business enterprise, one young man argued: "If I was in the same situation, I would definitely do it. I'd like to say that I wouldn't, but that would be lying, knowing true human nature." A female student replied, "If they offered me a certain amount of money, then I would."

When I inquired if they would draw the line on such behavior at a certain point, another student replied, "If it's a family member or just a close friend you would know—I just couldn't do it if I had to think of it in those terms. Any other terms, I would jump on it." Another young woman concurred: "If it wouldn't harm people that were relatives and family, I'd do it." Yet another student noted: "I would blackmail and do everything, but when it came to cheating on my husband or doing something that'll affect my family, I wouldn't do it."

At that point I asked if these students would engage in immoral practices as a last resort to keep their business functioning. Not one person in the class dissented. . . . While these students argued that their parents would censure such deeds, in "this world of dog eat dog," such deeds were, they added, "necessary."[13]

We recall our own experience. We too break rules, tell lies, hurt others. We find a student cheating on an examination. First, we hear the excuses. Soon we hear representative voices too: justifications, norms, and sympathies. Typically, at an event like a faculty or PTA meeting, we hear a series of monologues:

"I" know that "cheating is wrong" but "everyone does it." The first person speaks of expediency.

"Cheating is wrong" and must be punished. The third person pronounces the moral norm.

Yes, "cheating is wrong but. . . ." The second person asks for an appreciation of special circumstances but is not prepared to confuse explanation with justification.

Typically the student is punished and the monologues subside until the next time.

However, that is morally unsatisfactory because very little has happened to transform the players. Predictably, the next instance will be like this one, and will be talked about and dealt with in the same way. A tedious repetition comes to characterize the process of judgement. To get other things to happen, we may call attention to this state of affairs by pointing to the fact that we are not really addressing each other. We may remark that there is more than one cheater in our school, yet we all agree that cheating is wrong just as the students in the discussion agree that "selling drugs" or "dumping chemicals" is wrong. We point to conflicts between pretension and action. We are a nuisance, or as Socrates had it, a "gadfly." We wonder aloud to our colleagues in the lunchroom about what might have happened if the "faculty" really believed that cheating was wrong or if, in a show of solidarity, other students had admitted to cheating. More questions are heard; we find that we have company. Perhaps still nothing happens and we let it go . . . we are not ready, so we await the next occasion.

Teachers try to bring up doubts where there were none by using a story, a play, or a newspaper item. We may make an unexpected connection where there was none, such as between an event in class that we can "explain away" and a public event like the corruption of a public official that we cannot "explain away." Similarly, we may extend an argument to absurdity as by posing the Kantian question: "What if everyone did this?" If still greeted by indifference, we try to arouse attack and defense, challenging a common wisdom that condemns cheating, let us say, while condoning it in privileged groups like among our friends or by giving it a different name like "success." Thus, we are still opening with questions of meaning. Each of us had an assured position, but the questioning interrupts us. The classroom, after all, is not in the world, so dialogue is a permanent possibility on the grounds of good will between students and teachers.

Perhaps we propose an exercise, a shift of roles. Thus, a student who defended cheating is asked to speak with the voice of the law—to speak in the third person; another is asked to be an offender; a third is asked to integrate justice and mercy by being parent, teacher, or elder. Of course, students understand in a general way that they must avoid a conflict of interest, and they understand the fear of failure. They play the roles and manage to suppress their feelings. It is, after all, only play; but that is not quite the case; the play takes over. In speaking as the law, students also ask if something is wrong with it and with the violator too. We make sure that little is taken for granted. Playing the "law," the cheater, the judge, or the parent, students encounter themselves differently and take themselves seriously. Other participants, taking other roles, respond too. The various representative voices are heard.

As a dialogue evolves, we find ourselves with more than a single voice. We also find out that speaking is less important than listening. We take account of each other. Moral development is thus not a linear move from earlier to later, from lesser to greater inclusiveness, from concrete to abstract thinking. It is a thickening process in which we learn to be at home with the voices of a dialogue.

Thus far, however, a dialogue lacks direction. Self-doubt may only be psychological and discourse only a game. We get to moral doubt when we ask what we have violated or what good we intend. Our answers cannot merely report personal preferences or community norms and social rules. These only reflect tastes or conventions or politics. The three voices exhibit only what is—history, practice, and biography; but moral transformation is not just alteration, so we listen for a "fourth voice" that speaks to intention, that tells us when moral progress occurs.

Such an ideal voice transcends self, society, and community. Something there is in a dialogue that will not let it end in aimlessness. When we stop, we do not say, "So what?"[14] Perhaps we interpret this intervention of an ideal as the work of some Freudian "super-ego" or as a less psychologized equivalent like "conscience." These are representative voices to be sure, but they speak to actual collective moral judgements. In turn they are also judged as good or evil, but then we need a voice that lets us judge, so we listen for ways of judging the moral qualities of the judgement itself. When we hear a fourth voice, we are listening to that which is outside of society, community, or self.

This fourth voice is quite mysterious. To be sure, for a believer, it is the voice of God; and yet, even God may be judged. Socrates spoke of his "daemon," an inner voice that said "aye or nay," but even an inner voice must be assessed as trustworthy or not. A philosophic naturalist like John Dewey spoke of the "funded experience" of humankind, an ideal history. Functionally evident—a dialogue is incomplete without it—the fourth voice is ontologically obscure. Perhaps we need only recognize its aesthetic fittingness, the dramatic necessity of a fourth player. It makes moral demands and generates moral tensions in the other persons of the dialogue. Thus a dialogue teaches that moral choices are not simply matters of contract, treaty, or convention. A dialogue does not simply circle back on itself.

The fourth voice is embodied as an ideal person. Like the others, it too is transformed. Thus, the gods of the believer and the ideals of the philosophic naturalist may be said to mature. Often the fourth voice appears as the "stranger," a favorite device of dialogue. A character may speak in the voice of "conscience," a stranger within; as the voice of "history," a stranger on the landscape; or as the voice of "God," a stranger in the universe. It is the strangeness that is important.

This many-voiced description of a dialogue relies on the reflective activity we saw in the fifth curriculum. We are self-conscious, able to see ourselves seeing and think ourselves thinking. In a dialogue, reflection, which is a natural human capacity, is shaped into complicated practices. It takes form as it is embodied in characters, each experimenting as it were with different voices.[15]

V

Human beings are open to dialogue. Few of us merely play out the "roles" dictated by society. We add to them and integrate who we are with what we are said to be. Few of us simply retreat to egoism. We explain, justify, and excuse ourselves. By contrast, ordinary moral language is static and unimaginative. We codify norms. We expect, once the facts are established, to apply norms unambiguously to cases, and we look to community to "temper justice with mercy." We are all taught a moral routine that relies on a moral division of labor.

However, that is never adequate for the morally interesting situation, for the occasion when we are caught up in contradiction and conflict. For that we need moral education; we need to step aside into a dialogue. We come into the classroom to learn the moves from *talking at* to *talking to* to *talking with*; and then, differently equipped, we are forced back into the world by the dialogue itself. The doubting, the questioning includes "Will it work?" "How will it work?" and "Will it work better?" We try out ourselves and our ideas in the world once again.

Encounters thereby become psychosocial facts and have moral consequences. Other ways of teaching—exposition, explanation, description, demonstration, analysis—are easily encapsulated so that the classroom experience and the worldly experience remain unconnected except through specialized skills exercised in narrow channels. We know engineers who have studied history but who leave history and engineering unconnected, lawyers who are philosophical but who comfortably isolate law from reflection, and we know academics who leave wisdom behind each day in the academy.

Surely enough goes on in the lives of students, teachers, families, and society to invite us into a dialogue, but, again, we need not wait on the event. We may create the encounter with attention to our needs, personal and social. That is why in a society where private goals are near idolatry, we may make a special point of community service, student government, and peer counseling. These varieties of experience together with those that emerge in the second curriculum from the implicit moral life of institutions and structures can be transformed in the fifth curriculum. It is never enough simply to do these things, we must do them well, and that means that we must be able to say why we are doing them well. Reflection complements action. As a high-school student reported,

"Student-to-Student" [STS] is a way of working with other kids. . . . [It] was founded nearly three years ago to develop a greater sense of community and increased contact between older and younger students and to teach leadership techniques. . . .

Last year, the program was broadened to include an orientation program for new students, discussion groups for all students, and more activities for . . . homerooms. This year, in addition to the extra-curricular format, STS has been offered as a course.

[T]he course is an unusual one in that the students devote two of their four classes a week to teaching health education to [8th grade] ethics classes . . . the students learn about the topics themselves, help plan the [8th grade] classes, and then teach the classes, presenting information, role playing and holding open discussions.[16]

The next step, as yet untaken, is to move toward reflection, toward what we may even call a "philosophy" of service and of institutions.

Any morally interesting situation is fertile ground for dialogue. We need but listen for moral dissonance and search for the question that can transform monologue into encounter.[17] Interesting questions arise because we are violators able to understand that we are violated; judges forced to admit complicity; parents confessing ambivalence. Interesting questions begin as a revelation to ourselves. To return one last time to cheating: we ask why we construct an environment of competitions which invite it, or we ask why we praise cooperation while turning academic success into a war of each against all.

We are ready for a dialogue because we are always with other people. Thus, quite naturally, we move into other roles, speak with other voices. We are mimics and scene stealers, and in a classroom where reflection is invited, a dialogue offers a safe environment for experimenting with empathy. Hence we are in position to learn the interactions of reflection, reason, passion, and compassion.

The Socratic figure, whom we encounter in the classroom, forces us to stumble particularly when things are going smoothly. In this way, we can understand our frustration with good teaching. The death of Socrates is a parable about schooling at its best, but morally interesting situations continue to happen, so the death of Socrates does not end the matter. We are successors. Once we commit to a dialogue, we all take on something of the character of a teacher. Socrates lives on in his students: we all learn to shift to the perspectives of our moral opponents, to introduce the law when opportunism or sentimentality tempts us to ignore it; even to attack the law itself for the sake of what we call a "higher law." We learn to be wary when we hear voices that seem only to meet our prejudices. We work to insure the sounds of moral counterpoint.[18]

Dialogue is thus self-sustaining. It has its limitations, too. The world needs closure, has a rightful place for commitment and faith, but that is the world. In the classroom we invite many voices, so we expect moral education to be permanently unsettled. The voices of the dialogue will always be overheard in uncompleted conversations, but then, many interesting questions taste of dialogue. The sciences emerged from dogma when they surrendered finality; the arts depart the cliche when they try unexplored tones, shades, and shapes. So too it is with moral education when it leaves the protections of certainty. To recognize the persistence and presence of the morally interesting question is to call for building a classroom that can understand it. That undertaking, finally, marks our path away from the "well-behaved" student and invites us all to try ourselves in the art of the dialogue.

Notes

1. The notion of the problem and the problematic owes much to John Dewey's analysis of inquiry. "Reconstruction" was a typical description of the work of inquiry, as in his *Reconstruction in Philosophy* (New York: Henry Holt & Co., 1920). For a discussion of the idea of "habit," see Dewey's *Human Nature and Conduct* (New York: Holt, 1922).

2. Elizabeth Saenger, *Ethical Values, Lessons for Lower School Students (Grades 2-6)* (New York: Ethical Culture Schools, 1987), pp. 57-58.

3. See, for example, John Herman Randall, Jr., *Plato: Dramatist of the Life of Reason* (New York: Columbia University Press, 1970).

4. Edith Hamilton, *The Greek Way* (New York: W. W. Norton, 1983), pp. 87-88.

5. Shelley Berman, "Boston ESR/Dialogue Group," *Forum*, Educators For Social Responsibility 6, no. 1 (Summer 1987): 10.

6. Martin Heidegger, *Being and Time*, translated by John Marcquarrie and Edward Robinson (New York: Harper and Row, 1962), p. 208.

7. Peter Sommer, "Children As Historians," *Moral Education Forum* 8, no. 2 (Summer 1983): 36.

8. A reading of any available edition of Plato's *Dialogues* will illustrate this point.

9. See, in particular, Plato's *Apology* and *Republic*.

10. In thinking about the 1960s in the United States, I would suggest that the erosion of primary ties (family, tribe, and ethnicity) had a good deal to do with the either/or politics of the period. Equally interesting were the almost compulsive attempts to generate "community" without recognizing that community evolves and cannot simply be put in place by fiat or desire.

11. Without accepting Martin Buber's mysticism, it is nevertheless possible to benefit from his phenomenological discussion of "thou" as mediating the harshness of ego and experience. See his *I and Thou*, translated by Ronald Gregor Smith (New York: Scribner, 1958).

12. Those who have followed discussions of moral development have, as it were, chosen sides over the question of whether "justice" or "caring" as primary

virtues are in some senses gender-related. I suggest that the supposed opposition of justice and caring reflects the fact that the moral voices are more complex than either of the above views admits, and that the processes of moral development are better understood as dialectical. In a dialogue, of course, multiple stances are inevitable, and contradiction is only an invitation to development. See Carol Gilligan, *In a Different Voice* (Cambridge, Mass.: Harvard, 1982), and Lawrence Kohlberg, *The Philosophy of Moral Development*, vol. 1 (San Francisco: Harper and Row, 1981).

13. Herbert London, "What TV Drama Is Teaching our Children," *The New York Times*, Arts and Leisure section, August 23, 1987, p. 25.

14. In ethics, the problematic relationship of "is" and "ought" continues to puzzle theorists. The "fourth person," the stranger, is in that context an embodiment of "ought," but as embodiment it cannot be thought of as purely apart. Dialectically, the fourth voice is forced into dramatic interaction with the other three, and so it too responds, as it were, to the "is." The back and forth movement is reminiscent, in part, of John Rawls's notion of "reflective equilibrium." See his *Theory of Justice* (Cambridge, Mass.: Harvard, 1971), p. 20.

15. Reflection is part of the recent discussion of the improvement of teaching. A brief summary of some of the research may be found in Gerald W. Bracey, "Reflective Teachers," *Phi Delta Kappan* 69 (November 1987): 233-34.

16. Laura Goldberger, "Student to Student Program," *Ethics in Education* 4, no. 4 (March 1985): 6.

17. Lawrence Kohlberg, in describing advanced moral "stages," refers to "moral musical chairs." The ability to take another's position is a sign of moral development. My interest is only partly described by that sense of things. Equally as suggestive to me is what Thomas Kuhn refers to as a "paradigm shift" when he discusses the sciences, and which I would think might well be helpful in discussing ethics. See Kuhn's *Structure of Scientific Revolutions* (Chicago: University of Chicago Press, 1970).

18. Putting "stage" theory and dialogue together permits us to glimpse a notion of moral development that is closer to experience and less abstractly organized around the research needs of psychology.

Bibliography

Bellah, Robert N., et al. *Habits of the Heart*. New York: Harper and Row, 1985.

Berkowitz, M. W., and F. Oser, eds., *Moral Education: Theory and Practice*. Hillsdale, New Jersey: Erlbaum, 1985.

Dewey, John. *Democracy and Education*. 1916. Reprint. New York: Free Press, 1966.

———. *Experience, Nature, and Freedom*. Edited by Richard J. Bernstein. Indianapolis: Bobbs-Merrill, 1960.

———. *Human Nature and Conduct*. New York: Holt, 1922.

———. *Intelligence in the Modern World*. Edited by Joseph Ratner. New York: Modern Library, 1939.

Durkheim, Emile. *Moral Education. A Study in the Theory and Application of the Sociology of Education*. New York: Free Press, 1973.

Elkind, David. *The Hurried Child*. Reading, Mass.: Addison-Wesley, 1981.

Erikson, Erik. *Childhood and Society*. New York: Norton, 1963.

Freud, Sigmund. *Civilization and Its Discontents*. Translated and edited by James Strachey. New York: Norton, 1961.

Friere, Paulo. *Philosophy of the Oppressed*. New York: Seabury, 1973.

Fromm, Erich. *Escape from Freedom*. New York: Rhinehart and Company, 1941.

Gardner, Howard. *Frames of Mind: The Theory of Multiple Intelligences*. New York: Basic Books, 1985.

Gilligan, Carol. *In a Different Voice*. Cambridge, Mass.: Harvard, 1982.

Giroux, H., and D. Purpel, eds. *The Hidden Curriculum and Moral Education*. Berkeley, Calif.: McCutchan, 1983.

Greene, Maxine. *Landscapes of Learning*. New York: Teachers College, 1978.

Hook, Sidney, P. Kurtz, and M. Todorovich, eds., *The Philosophy of the Curriculum*. Buffalo: Prometheus Press, 1975.

Illich, Ivan. *De-Schooling Society.* New York: Harper and Row, 1970.

Jaeger, Werner. *Paideia: The Ideals of Greek Culture.* 3 vols. Translated by Gilbert Highet. New York: Oxford, 1945.

Kohlberg, Lawrence. *Collected Papers on Moral Development and Moral Education.* 2 vols. Cambridge, Mass.: Harvard, 1975.

––––– . *Essays on Moral Development.* Vol. 1 *The Philosophy of Moral Development.* San Francisco: Harper and Row, 1981.

Kuhn, Thomas. *The Structure of Scientific Revolutions.* Chicago: University of Chicago Press, 1962.

Lickona, Thomas. *Raising Good Children.* New York: Bantam, 1983.

Lippman, Matthew, A. Sharp, and F. Oscanyan. *Philosophy in the Classroom:* Philadelphia: Temple University Press, 1980.

MacIntyre, Alasdair. *After Virtue.* Indiana: Notre Dame, 1981.

Matthews, Gareth. *Philosophy and the Young Child.* Cambridge, Mass.: Harvard, 1984.

Mosher, Ralph, ed. *Moral Education: A First Generation of Research and Development.* New York: Praeger, 1980.

Moynihan, Daniel Patrick. *Family and Nation.* New York: Harcourt Brace and Jovanovich, 1986.

Noddings, Nell. *Caring, a Feminine Approach to Ethics and Moral Education.* Berkeley, Calif.: University of California Press, 1984.

Piaget, Jean. *The Essential Piaget.* Edited by H. E. Gruber and J. J. Voneche. New York: Basic Books, 1977.

––––– . *The Moral Judgement of the Child.* New York: Free Press, 1965.

Piatelli-Palmarini, M. *Language and Learning (The Debate Between Jean Piaget and Noam Chomsky).* Cambridge, Mass.: Harvard, 1980.

Plato. *The Dialogues of Plato.* 2 vols. Translated by Benjamin Jowett. New York: Random House, 1937.

Purpel, D., and K. Ryan, eds. *Moral Education . . . It Comes with the Territory.* Berkeley, Calif.: McCutchan, 1976.

Raths, Louis, Merrill Harmin, and Sidney Simon. *Values and Teaching.* Columbus, Ohio: Charles E. Merrill, 1966.

Rawls, John. *A Theory of Justice.* Cambridge, Mass.: Harvard, 1971.

Reimer, Joseph, D. P. Paolitto, and R. H. Hersh. *Promoting Moral Growth.* New York: Longman, 1983.

Ryan, Kevin, and George McClean, eds., *Character Development in Schools and Beyond.* New York: Praeger, 1987.

Saenger, Elizabeth. *Ethical Values (Lessons for Lower School Students, Grades 2-6).* New York: Ethical Culture Schools, 1987.

Scharf, Peter, ed. *Readings in Moral Education.* Winston, 1977.

Schulman, Michael, and Eva Mekler. *Bringing up a Moral Child.* Reading, Mass.: Addison-Wesley, 1985.

Simon, Sidney, and J. Clarke. *More Values Clarification.* Renant, 1975.

Sizer, Theodore. *Horace's Compromise.* Boston: Houghton Mifflin, 1984.

Skinner, B. F. *Beyond Freedom and Dignity.* New York: Knopf, 1971.

Traviss, Sister Mary Peter, OP. *Student Moral Development in the Catholic School.* NCEA Keynote Series. Washington, D.C.: National Catholic Education Association, 1985.

Weinstein, Mark, ed. with Beatrice Banu. *The Fieldston Ethics Reader.* Washington, D.C.: University Press of America, 1988.

Williams, Bernard. *Ethics and the Limits of Philosophy.* Cambridge, Mass.: Harvard, 1985.

Wynne, Edward, ed. *Character Policy: An Emerging Issue.* Washington, D.C.: University Press of America, 1982.

Index

About the Author

HOWARD B. RADEST is director of the Ethical Culture/Fieldston Schools of New York and chair of the ethics department. Previously he was professor of philosophy, Ramapo College, and executive director of the American Ethical Union. He founded and chairs the University Seminar on Moral Education at Columbia University, is a member of the Advisory Board of the Association for Moral Education, and is on the editorial boards of several periodicals and professional journals. He edited *To Seek a Humane World* and *Understanding Ethical Religion*, and authored *Toward Common Ground*, which is now in a second edition.